Orthodox Christian Bible Commentary

HEBREWS

By His Eminence Metropolitan Youssef

Orthodox Christian Bible Commentary: Hebrews

Copyright © 2013 Coptic Orthodox Diocese of the Southern United States.

All rights reserved.

Designed & Published by:
St. Mary & St. Moses Abbey Press
101 S Vista Dr., Sandia, TX 78383
stmabbeypress.com

Printed in the United States of America

Library of Congress Control Number: 2013955076

Cover design image photo by Katherine Nawar,
and icon from Bedour Latif and Youssef Nassief.

All Scripture quotations, unless otherwise indicated, are taken from the New King James Version® Copyright © 1982 by Thomas Nelson, Inc. Used by permission. All rights reserved.

10 9 8 7 6 5 4 3 2

Contents

Introduction to Hebrews... 1

Chapter 1..7

Chapter 2..13

Chapter 3..21

Chapter 4..31

Chapter 5..41

Chapter 6..51

Chapter 7..63

Chapter 8..75

Chapter 9..85

Chapter 10..101

Chapter 11..121

Chapter 12..137

Chapter 13..149

Comparison Chart:

Day of Atonement and Christ's sacrifice... 158

St. Paul's Epistle to the Hebrews

AUTHOR: St. Paul. There was a consensus in the Early Church that St. Paul was the author, especially considering when he said, *"know that our brother Timothy has been set free, with whom I shall see you if he comes shortly"* (Hebrews 13: 22, 23). We know that Timothy was a close companion to St. Paul, so that no one could really say this other than St. Paul (see Phil. 2:20-22; 1 Tim. 1:2).

Some scholars reject St. Paul's authorship. They argue two main points. First, they note that St. Paul did not mention his name in this letter, unlike the thirteen other letters he wrote where he did mention his name. This is the only letter traditionally attributed to St. Paul that does not mention him by name. In response to this criticism, we say two things: (1) This letter was written, as is clear, to the Jews (the Hebrews). They considered St. Paul as one breaking the law of Moses because he taught against circumcision and the notion that Christians must keep Jewish tradition: *"but they have been informed about you that you teach all the Jews who are among the Gentiles to forsake Moses, saying that they ought not to circumcise their children, nor to walk according to the customs"* (Acts 21: 21). If St. Paul wrote his name in the beginning of the letter, they would not have read it. (2) Another reason why he did not mention his name is because St. Paul was the apostle to the Gentiles (Rom. 11:13; Gal. 2:7-8), not to the Jews. Therefore, when be wrote to the Hebrews, he did not command them as their apostle. You will notice in all the other letters where he wrote his name, he would usually begin by saying something like, "Paul, an apostle of Jesus Christ, to the church of" whomever he was addressing.

The second criticism why scholars say the author of this letter is not St. Paul is that St. Paul was not skilled in the Greek language, yet this letter was written in very sophisticated Greek. In response to this, St. Paul was a Hebrew, of the tribe of Benjamin; so why would he write this letter in Greek? It would make sense that he would write this letter in Hebrew, in which the original letter was written, and later it was translated into Greek.

PLACE & TIME: Before 65 A.D. In Hebrews 13:24, St. Paul says, *"those from Italy greet you."* The persecution in Rome, Italy carried out by Nero occurred about 65 AD, which was brought on by the fire that engulfed much of Rome. Therefore, it is most likely that the book of Hebrews was written before 65 AD, before the persecution that started in Rome, because this greeting is from the Christians in Italy, which suggests that there was peace there at the time of the writing of this letter.

CANONICITY

The epistle was accepted by the Early Church fathers (most of whom quoted from this letter) and the Ecumenical Councils as one of St. Paul's letters in the New Testament.

RECIPIENTS

This letter was written primarily to Jews who had converted to Christianity and who were familiar with the Old Testament, as evinced by the fact that he mentioned many things in this epistle that only Jews would understand (e.g., Melchizedek, the Temple, the Tabernacle, the Holy of Holies, the golden censer).

PURPOSE

The Jews were very proud of their traditions. *"Indeed you are called a Jew, and rest on the law, and make your boast in God"* (Rom. 2:17). The Jews boast that they received the law from angels (Acts 7:53) and through Moses, the man of God (Deut. 33:1). It was the only nation that had the Temple, prophets, sacrifices, and to whom God consistently spoke with directly (see Rom. 9:4-6). They had the tendency to want to return to their Judaism. Thus, St. Paul was trying to convince wavering Jewish Christians not to desert Christ and return to their former religion. St. Paul wanted to make sure they understood that Christianity is superior to Judaism. The message of this letter can be summed up in three words: "Christ is better."

There are five warnings against apostasy:
1. Danger of Neglect (2:1-4).
2. Danger of Unbelief (3:7-19).

3. Danger of Not Maturing (5:11-14).
4. Danger of Shrinking Back (10:26-39).
5. Danger of Refusing God (12:25:39).

Another reason St. Paul wrote this letter was to help both Jewish and Gentile Christians make sense out of the Old Testament, showing its relevance in a world influenced by Greek ideas. He wanted to connect the Old Testament with the New Testament, which St. Paul expounds upon in detail in this epistle.

THEME

The superiority of Christ and Christianity – Christ is superior. There is no person or being that is like Christ. This main over-arching theme was divided into three parts:
- The superiority of the person of Christ (Ch. 1-4)
- The superiority of Christ's work (Ch. 4-10)
- The superiority of our privileges as Christians (Ch. 10-13)

OUTLINE OF HEBREWS

Chapter 1
- God revealing Himself (1-3)
- Christ, superior to the angels (4-14)

Chapter 2
- First warning: danger of neglect (1-4)
- Christ's superiority to the angels (5-9)
- Jesus is the pioneer of salvation (10-18)
- A merciful and faithful High Priest (16-18)

Chapter 3
- Jesus is greater than Moses (1-6)
- Second warning: danger of unbelief—hardening of the heart (7-11)
Keep from being hardened by sin's deceitfulness (12-14)
- Unbelief made it impossible to enter God's rest (15-19)

Chapter 4
- Be sure to enter the promised rest (1-11)
- The living, powerful word of God (12-13)
- Our sympathetic High Priest (14-16)

Chapter 5
- The qualifications of the high priest (1-4)

- Christ's qualifications for the high priesthood (5-10)
- Third warning: dullness of hearing (11-14)

Chapter 6
- A call to perfection (1-3)
- The danger of apostasy (4-8)
- Encouragement to persevere (9-12)
- God's promise is steadfast (13-20)

Chapter 7
- Melchizedek the high priest (1-10)
- The eternal priesthood of Christ (11-25)
- The ultimate uniqueness of Christ (26-28)

Chapter 8
- Heavenly sanctuary (1-5)
- Better covenant (6-13)

Chapter 9
- Worship in the old covenant—restricted access to God (1-10)
  - The Tabernacle (1-5)
  - Worship in the Tabernacle (6-10)
- Superior new covenant provides superior access to God in worship (11-28)
  - Christ entered by His own blood (11-14)
  - The Mediator of a new covenant (15-28)

Chapter 10
- Ineffectiveness of the Levitical Law (1-4)
- Sanctification through Christ's sacrifice (5-10)
- Christ the new High Priest (11-14)
- The adequacy of the new covenant (15-18)
- Call to use our access to God (19-25)
- Fourth warning: danger of shrinking back (26-31)
- The call to perseverance (32-39)

Chapter 11
- Definition of faith (1-3)
- Faith before the flood (4-7)
- The faith of the Patriarchs (8-22)
- The faith of Moses (13-29)
- Other examples of faith (30-38)
- The promise is Christ (39, 40)

Chapter 12
- Imitating the Lord (1-4)
- Discipline (5-11)
- The call to holiness (12-17)
- Pilgrimage of the new covenant (18-24)
- Danger of refusing God (25-29)

Chapter 13
- Love (1-7)
  - Brotherly love (1)
  - Love of strangers (2-3)
  - Love in marriage (4-6)
  - Love of pastors and shepherds (7)

- Warning against heretics (8-9)
- Christian sacrifices (10-16)
- Exhortations and benediction (17-21)
- Final notes and remarks (22-25)

1

Chapter Outline

- God revealing Himself (1-3)
- Christ, superior to the angels (4-14)

1:1-3 The main point here is that Christ is superior to those men through whom God revealed His message in the Old Testament. St. Paul was trying to tell the Jewish Christians who were thinking of returning to Judaism, "As a Jew, God spoke to you through the prophets, but as a Christian, God spoke to you through His Son, which shows you Christianity is superior to Judaism." (Note that beginning with this chapter and through the second, this is the Pauline reading of the Feast of the Nativity.)

God, who at various times and in various ways spoke in time past to the fathers by the prophets has in these last days spoken to us by His Son. In the Old Testament (*"in time past"*), God spoke to the Jews through the prophets who served as the agents of God's message. He spoke in *"various ways,"* sometimes speaking directly, and sometimes speaking indirectly (such as through dreams or through angels). God also spoke at *"various times,"* as there were times that God was silent, and other times that He chose to speak. But now in the New Testament, *"in these last days,"* God spoke through Christ, who is superior to those men through whom God revealed His message in the Old Testament. While in the Old Testament God spoke *"at various times and in various ways,"* in the New Testament Christ says, *"lo, I am with you always"* (Matt. 28:10); every day He is with us at the altar. While in the Old Testament God spoke through the prophets, we are privileged that God now speaks through His Son. The words of the Son have more weight than the words delivered by the prophets in time past because of Who He is. St. Paul described the Son in seven ways:

whom He has appointed heir of all things. (1 of 7) It is natural, then, that the Son, as both God and man, is the heir of all things. Our goal is to inherit the kingdom of God. As servants, we cannot inherit it. It is only through uniting with the only begotten Son that we can enter the kingdom of God. Prophets cannot inherit the kingdom of God because they are only servants. When we are united with the Son, our status will change from servants to children, because we will be the bride of the Son. If you have servants, and you have one son; if he marries one of the female servants in your house, then her status will change from being a servant to being a daughter-in-law who is now eligible to inherit from the father of her husband. As St. Paul said, *"if children, then heirs—heirs of God and joint heirs with Christ"* (Rom. 8:17).

We are privileged because God speaks to us through the Son who is the heir of all things. If the sons of Abraham hoped to be heirs of the Promised Land, the sons of God in Christ can hope to be heirs of the whole universe.

through whom also He made the worlds. (2 of 7) He said the *"worlds"* (plural), speaking of the earth and the heavens (including the invisible creation). In the Old Testament, God spoke through His prophets, who were His creation. But in the New Testament, God spoke through Christ, the creator Himself, who created the universe, together with the Father and the Holy Spirit. Therefore, Christ co-created with the Father, and the Holy Spirit, and was also the agent of creation—God created by His Word, who is the Logos of the Father.

who being the brightness of His glory. (3 of 7) Think about the sun and its light. If there is no light that comes from the sun, can we see it? No. But, through the light that comes from the sun, we are able to see it. Christ is the brightness of the glory of the Father. As we cannot separate the light from the Sun, we cannot separate the Son from the Father. The light is born from the Sun, as the Son is begotten, not created, from the Father. St. Athanasius used Heb. 1:1-4 to prove to Arius that Christ did not have a beginning; His true essential nature was of God. In the Nicene Creed, it proclaims Christ as *"Light of Light."* As the sun does not exist without radiating light, so the Father does not exist without the Son. Thus, the Son reflects His Father's glory in this world. The unapproachable light of divinity is approachable only in the incarnated Christ. Through the Son, we can see the Father: (*"Philip said to Him, 'Lord, show us the Father, and it is sufficient for us.' Jesus said to him, '... He who has seen Me has seen the Father ... I am in the Father and the Father in Me'"*—John 14:8-11).

and the express image of His person. (4 of 7) The essence of the Son is the same as the essence of the Father. As we say in the Orthodox Creed, *"of one essence with the Father."* The Son is our true God, so we are privileged that God speaks to us through His Son, the divine God, not just through human prophets as in the Old Testament.

and upholding all things by the word of His power. (5 of 7) Many times a factory can make a machine but does not know how to preserve it and maintain it. However, God is able to sustain His creation, preserve the universe, and has absolute authority over it. Imagine if God's mercy over the world was taken for just a fraction of a second. This whole world is preserved by the Son.

when He had by Himself purged our sins. (6 of 7) God is seen as an untouchable superior in other religions. St. Paul just spoke so highly of Christ, exalting Him above all; but then he draws our attention to how our God in Christianity is different: When we sinned, God did not feel ashamed to empty Himself and to become a man in order to save us and to redeem us. St. Paul wants to demonstrate the humility of the Son and the greatness of His love. He *"made Himself of no reputation, taking the form of a bondservant, and coming in the likeness of men"* (Phil. 2:6), **sat down at the right hand of the Majesty on high.** (7 of 7) After conquering sin and death, the Son, as a man, is exalted, sitting at the right hand of the Father. God elevated Him after He finished His mission. He returned to His glory as a judge and co-ruler of the world.

THE SUPERIORITY OF CHRIST	ABOVE THE PROPHETS In verses 1-3, St. Paul describes seven ways the Son is superior to the prophets.	ABOVE THE ANGELS In verses 4-14, St. Paul uses verses from the Old Testament to reiterate how the same seven aspects of the Son make him superior to the angels.
(1) He is the Son.	"heir of all things" (v.2)	"For to which of the angels did He ever say: 'You are My Son, Today I have begotten You'? And again: 'I will be to Him a Father, And He shall be to Me a Son'?" (v.5)
(2) & (3) He is the Lord and King.	"the brightness of His glory and the express image of His person" (v.3)	"Your throne, O God, is forever and ever; A scepter of righteousness is the scepter of Your kingdom." (v.8)
(4) He is the Christ, the Anointed, who purified our sins.	"when He had by Himself purged our sins" (v.3)	"Therefore God, Your God, has anointed You with the oil of gladness more than Your companions." (v.9)
(5) He is the Creator.	"through whom also He made the worlds" (v.2)	"You, LORD, in the beginning laid the foundation of the earth, And the heavens are the work of Your hands." (v.10)
(6) He is the Pantocrator.	"upholding all things by the word of His power" (v.3)	"They will perish, but You remain; and they will all grow old like a garment; Like a cloak You will fold them up, and they will be changed. But You are the same, and Your years will not fail." (v.11-12)
(7) He is the Ruler.	"sat down at the right hand of the Majesty on high" (v.3)	"But to which of the angels has He ever said: 'Sit at My right hand, till I make Your enemies Your footstool'? Are they not all ministering spirits sent forth to minister for those who will inherit salvation?" (v.13-14)

1:4 having become so much better than the angels, as He has by inheritance obtained a more excellent name than they. St. Paul speaks to the Jewish Christians who want to return to Judaism. After he addressed one source of pride (that they received the message of God through the prophets) by explaining that Christians receive the message of God from Christ, the Incarnate Son, he then addresses another point of Jewish pride. They boasted in the fact that they received the Old Testament through angels: *"who have received the law by the direction of angels and have not kept it"* (Acts 7:53). But St. Paul wants to make clear to them that Christ is superior to angels, and so they should be even more proud of that fact. Therefore, the second illustration of Christ's superiority compares Him to the angels. *"He* [Christ] *by inheritance"* [because He is the Son of the Father] *has obtained a more excellent name* [*"name"*—referring to the whole person, character, and nature of Christ: His whole being] *than they."* To prove his point, St. Paul takes seven quotes from the Old Testament (which would be persuasive to his audience who are Jews, familiar with the Old Testament, and who converted to Christianity):

1:5 For to which of the angels did He ever say: "You are My Son, Today I have begotten You"? And again: "I will be to Him a Father, And He shall be to Me a Son"? (1 of 7) Christ is superior to the angels because while the angels are merely servants of God, He is the Son of God and thus, the heir to the throne of God. No angel was ever called God's Son. God the Father addressed the Son in these verses, the first of which is from Psalm 2:7 and the second is taken from 2 Samuel 7:14.

1:6 But when He again brings the firstborn into the world. The *"firstborn"* is the Son, the Lord Jesus Christ. Sometimes the Jehovah's witnesses use this verse to say that since Christ is referred to in this way, then He is not equal to the Father. Our response to this is, St. Paul did not say Christ is the "first creation" but rather said, He is the *"firstborn."* He is not created by the Father, but is begotten from Him. We say that the Son is born, begotten of the Father before all ages; but He is begotten in a mysterious way without any time difference—as eternal as God is, so too is Christ. As the light is begotten from the Sun while there is no real time difference that can be detected, in a similar way Christ is begotten of the Father before all ages.

He says: "Let all the angels of God worship Him." A second contrast which proves Christ's superiority, is the fact that He is worshipped by the angels. This verse is in Deuteronomy 32:43 of the Septuagint (if you look at your Bibles, you may find this verse to be different, but this translation is taken from the Septuagint—the Greek translation of the Hebrew Bible, which is the authorized version of the Old Testament in the Orthodox Church, and is the version from which the Early Church Fathers quoted exclusively, as well as the writers in the New Testament, including St. Paul). If Christ is worshipped by the angels, then He must be superior to them. The Son is superior to the angels because He is the creator and the angels are His creation.

1:7-8 And of the angels He says: "Who makes His angels spirits and His ministers a flame of fire." But to the Son He says: "Your throne, O God, is forever and ever; A scepter of righteousness is the scepter of Your kingdom. (2 & 3 of 7) The angels are just spirits and a flame of fire (Ps. 104:4), but the Son is Lord and King (*"throne"* and *"scepter"*—Ps. 45:6, 7).

1:9 **God.** Referring to the person of the Father.

Your God. Christ is spoken to in this verse, and it is said to Him, "Your God," because the Son became a man and brother to us all.

has anointed You with the oil of gladness. (4 of 7) "Christ" means the anointed one. St. Paul says, He is the Christ, the anointed one to become the King, the Priest, the Prophet (as throughout the Old Testament priests, kings, and prophets were anointed with oil). No angel received such an anointing.

Your companions. This refers to the angels.

1:10 And: "You, LORD, in the beginning laid the foundation of the earth, And the heavens are the work of Your hands. (5 of 7) He is the creator of the worlds (heaven and earth—see 1:3).

1:11-12 They will perish, but You remain; And they will all grow old like a garment; Like a cloak You will fold them up, and they will be changed. But You are the same, And Your years will not fail." (6 of 7) God is the Pantocrator, the sustainer of the universe. He is unchangeable and immutable.

1:13-14 But to which of the angels has He ever said: "Sit at My right hand, Till I make Your enemies Your footstool"? Are they not all ministering spirits sent forth to minister for those who will inherit salvation? (7 of 7) Sitting at the right hand of the Father means that He is the ruler, while the angels are just ministering spirits.

Chapter 1 Questions

1. What overall picture of Christ emerges immediately when reading the first four verses?

2. Verse 5 quotes from Psalm 2:7 and 2 Samuel 7:14. Find those verses and read the surrounding verses. What other insights into Christ to you receive from those Old Testament passages?

3. If, as verse 6 states, angels worship Christ, what should our daily response to our Lord be?

4. Verses 8 and 9 quote from Psalm 45. Read Psalm 45 and discover the verses there that are quoted. What does Saint Paul find in Psalm 45 that causes him to apply it to Christ?

5. What common elements do you discover between Psalm 45 and Isaiah 61:1-11?

6. The idea that creation was made by Him (our Lord Jesus Christ) and by His Word is also found in John 1:1-5 and Colossians 1:15-20. Read those passages and think about why it was important for the New Testament to describe Jesus as being involved in the Creation of the world. Jot down some of your ideas.

2

Chapter Outline

- First warning: danger of neglect (1-4)
- Christ's superiority to the angels (5-9)
- Jesus is the pioneer of salvation (10-18)
- A merciful and faithful High Priest (16-18)

2:1 Therefore we must give the more earnest heed to the things we have heard, lest we drift away. St. Paul is saying we must pay attention to the word of God, which we received from Christ—the words of the New Testament. The message of Christ is salvation. Hence, we should *"give the more earnest heed"* to the message of salvation *"lest we drift away."* There are five warnings given in the book of Hebrews against apostasy. This is the first: the danger of drifting away (neglect). This brings to mind the image of a drifting boat. If a boat is not anchored to something strong, then it will drift away, little by little, without much notice; eventually it will end up far gone and will not be salvageable anymore. We must pay careful attention to Christ's word lest we drift away. Drifting is dangerous, because it does not happen all at once. It happens very slowly and gradually. Moreover, because it is gradual, it often goes unnoticed until it is too late. Everyday, if we do not pay attention to Christ's message, because of the cares and desires of the world, we will find ourselves completely away from Christ. In (Hebrews 6:19), we shall see that we have an anchor of the soul: Jesus Christ: *"This hope we have as an anchor of the soul, both sure and steadfast, and which enters the Presence behind the veil."* The Jewish Christians had anchored their hopes to the Temple and its rituals and sacrifices, but Christians should solely attach themselves to Christ.

2:2-4 For if the word spoken through angels. The Jews boasted in the fact they received the Old Testament through angels: *"who have received the law by the direction of angels and have not kept it"* (Acts 7:53). This *"word spoken through angels"* refers to the Old Testament.

proved steadfast. Truly the words of God in the Old Testament have proved steadfast: *"Heaven and earth will pass away, but My words will by no means pass away"* (Matt. 24:35; Mark 13:31; Luke 21:33).

and every transgression and disobedience received a just reward. how shall we escape if we neglect so great a salvation, which at the first began to be spoken by the Lord, and was confirmed to us by those who heard Him. In the Old Testament every transgression was punished. If the law, which was the message spoken by angels, was enforced, then how much more should we pay attention to the message given by the Son; certainly the superior revelation of Jesus Christ will also be enforced. It is paramount that we do not neglect the message of Christ. The answer to St. Paul's question, "how shall we escape" is simple: we will not be able to.

which at the first began to be spoken by the Lord, and was confirmed to us by those who heard Him, God also bearing witness both with signs and wonders, with various miracles, and gifts of the Holy Spirit, according to His own will? St. Paul gives a description of the message of the New Testament. First, this message was declared by the Lord Jesus Christ. Second, this message was affirmed and delivered to us by the apostles who heard Him. Third, this message was accompanied by many powerful signs, wonders, miracles, and gifts of the Holy Spirit. Since this powerful message has been delivered in such an extraordinary way, the neglect of this message, which leads to drifting away, is inexcusable.

2:5 For He has not put the world to come, of which we speak, in subjection to angels. This refers to the eternal life, *"the age to come"* (Matt. 12:32; Mark 10:30; Luke 18:30), the *"new heaven"* and *"new earth"* (Rev. 21:1). There was a belief among the Jewish Christians that the current world in which we are living right now is under the subjection of the angels. So the argument by St. Paul here is, God did not entrust the world to come, the eternal life, to be under the subjection of the angels, but He gave it to the Son. When the Lord Jesus Christ started His ministry, He preached the kingdom of God, eternal life, which was a clear announcement that the coming world had arrived with His ministry. Christ told the people, *"the kingdom of God is at hand, repent"* (Mark 1:15), which means it is under his power and authority. So, if the Father entrusted the Son with the world to come, then the Son is superior to the angels. He supports his argument with the following verses.

2:6 But one testified in a certain place, saying. This *"one"* who *"testfied"* refers to David the prophet, because from this verse to verse 8, St. Paul quotes the Septuagint version (Greek translation of the Hebrew Bible, quoted by all the Early Church fathers, as well as the New Testament writers) of Psalm 8:4-6.

"What is man that You are mindful of him, Or the son of man that You take care of him? Why did St. Paul quote King David here? He is saying, we humans are just dust and ashes, just God's creation, so who are we that God pays attention to us. This reflects God's love for us, although we are simply *"dust and ashes"* (as Abraham said about himself—Gen. 18:27; also, *"for dust you are, and to dust"*—Gen. 3:19).

2:7 You have made him a little lower than the angels; You have crowned him with glory and honor, And set him over the works of Your hands. He switches from the fallen humanity to speaking about the perfect man, who is the Lord Jesus Christ, who was incarnated and became man for our salvation. Definitely, through the incarnation, through the suffering of Christ, and through His humiliation, He was made a little lower than the angels. More accurately, the Septuagint translation reads, *"You have made him, for a little time, lower than the angels."* This phrase *"little time"* means that Christ, for a little period of time (during His period when He was incarnate), was made lower than the angels through His suffering. Now, through His resurrection and ascension into the heavens, He sits at the right hand of the Father and is crowned with glory and honor (as explained previously in 1:3, 13-14).

2:8 You have put all things in subjection under his feet." For in that He put all in subjection under Him, He left nothing that is not put under Him. In this psalm, David prophesied about the Messiah, that the Father set the Son over all the works of His hands, which is also the works of the Son (because God created the world by the Son—see 1:2, 10; John 1:3). The psalm says very clearly that *"all things"* have been put under subjection to Christ. Thus, St. Paul reflects on this psalm and reiterates that, "He left nothing that is not put under Him."

But now we do not yet see all things put under Him. While all things are subject to Christ, at present, in this world, simple observation shows that not all things are subject to Him at present. In this world currently, we do not see that everything is under the Son. As we read in 1 Corinthians 15:24-28, we read about many enemies (many things) that are not yet subjected to the Son (e.g., *"The last enemy that will be destroyed is death"*—1 Cor. 15:26). And here St. Paul is making the argument that, if in the current world not everything is under His subjection, then when will this be fulfilled? Not in the current world, but in the age to come. Thus, King David's prophesy is a prophecy about the age to come, which is given to Christ. Therefore, God the Father did not entrust the angels with the administration of the world to come—then, Christ is superior to the angels.

2:9 But we see Jesus, who was made a little lower than the angels, for the suffering of death crowned with glory and honor. The Lord Jesus Christ, who was made lower than the angels through His suffering and crucifixion (2:7), is now *"crowned with glory and honor."* There is a lesson for us here: all of us would like to be glorified with the Lord, but we cannot unless we *"suffer with Him, that we may also be glorified together"* (Rom. 8:17).

by the grace of God. This gift of salvation was given to us by the grace of God (see Rom. 3:24; Titus 3:7). It is not because we are worthy, but because God loved us. *"But God, who is rich in mercy, because of His great love with which He loved us, even when we were dead in trespasses, made us alive together with Christ (by grace you have been saved)"* (Eph. 2:4-5); *"And walk in love, as Christ also has loved us and given Himself for us, an offering and a sacrifice to God for a sweet-smelling aroma"* (Eph. 5:2); *"Now may our Lord Jesus Christ Himself, and our God and Father, who has loved us and given us everlasting consolation and good hope by grace"* (2 Th. 2:16); *"In this is love, not that we loved God, but that He loved us and sent His Son to be the propitiation for our sins"* (1 John 4:10); *"... To Him who loved us and washed us from our sins in His own blood"* (Rev. 1:5).

that He ... might taste death for everyone. That is what we call "substitution" (*"For He made Him who knew no sin to be sin for us, that we might become the righteousness of God in Him"*—1 Cor. 5:21). He died on our behalf, instead of us, which is the concept of atonement. The reason for His incarnation, humiliation, suffering, and death was so that He would die instead of us. He took my sins in His body and became a ransom for the world: *"the Son of Man did not come to be served, but to serve, and to give His life a ransom for many"* (Matt. 20:28; Mark 10:45); *"who gave Himself a ransom for all, to be testified in due time"* (1 Tim. 2:6).

2:10-18 St. Paul began to introduce another concept about the Lord Jesus Christ (after introducing the concept of Christ being superior to angels as previously mentioned). Now he is trying to reflect on Christ as the High Priest. During the Old Testament, the high priest was very honored. St. Paul will compare how Christ is the High Priest according to the order of Melchizedek, while all other high priests were according to the order of Levi and Aaron.

2:10 For it was fitting for Him. Many people ask, why did God not save us in a different way? Why did he save us through the crucifixion of the Son. St. Paul says that it was fitting for Him (referring to the Father). The incarnation was the proper and only way of resolving the problem of fallen humanity. St. Athanasius, in his book "The Incarnation of the Logos" explains in detail why this was the only means to effectuate salvation.

for whom are all things and by whom are all things. St. Paul is saying that God created us by Him and for Him. So, we find meaning in our humanity only in our relationship with God. Away from God, there is no meaning for my humanity, and no fulfillment of my being. That is why St. Paul wants to say that the human being finds meaning and fulfillment in a covenant relationship with God.

in bringing many ... to glory. This refers to the redemption of our fallen nature, to restore the image and likeness of God that we lost due to the fall of Adam. God the Father, through the Lord Jesus Christ, became involved in leading us to glory. That is why we say in the praises, "through the good pleasure of the Father, He was incarnate." This refers to the concept of redemption, which is the process of restoring our fallen race to the original glory and likeness of God's image (Gen. 1:27).

sons. We are sons by adoption, not by nature. Christ is the Son by nature (Light of Light, true God of true God, as is said in the Orthodox Creed). As explained previously, we are heirs through our union with Christ, regarded as children rather than servants because we are Christ's bride. If you have servants, and you have one son, if he marries one of the female servants in your house, then her status will change from being a servant to being a daughter-in-law who is now eligible to inherit from the father of her husband. We are like that servant girl, having been wed to Christ.

captain of their salvation. This refers to Christ, and because He is our captain, then we should follow His lead and direction. He became man and became the leader of mankind, bringing us all into salvation.

perfect through sufferings. This does not mean that Christ was not perfect before His sufferings. He was, is, and will forever be perfect ("Jesus Christ is the same yesterday, today, and forever."—Heb. 13:8). To make Him perfect means to finish the mission and the goal of His incarnation. The last words spoken by Christ on the cross were, *"it is finished"* (John 19:30). To achieve salvation for mankind, Christ had to suffer. Since Christ is our captain, then following His steps will make us perfect through suffering too.

2:11 **For both He who sanctifies and those who are being sanctified are all of one, for which reason He is not ashamed to call them brethren.** St. Paul continues to draw our attention to the concept of the priesthood of the Lord Jesus Christ. St. Paul is stressing Christ's close identification with us as humans, and emphasizing Christ's priestly role. For Christ, who sanctifies us, and we who are being sanctified by Him, are all of the same family (all of one). Since we share the same Father as Christ, we are, in this sense, Christ's brothers and family. Christ is not ashamed to call us brothers.

2:12-13 **saying: "I will declare Your name to My brethren; In the midst of the assembly I will sing praise to You."** In this quote from Psalm 22:22, we find the Son, Jesus Christ, saying to the Father, *"I will declare Your name to My brethren."* We are Christ's brethren, sharing the same Father as Christ. The family concept here is very clear. Christ is saying, "In the midst of the assembly (the family of God), I will sing praise to God the Father." We say this in the Divine Liturgy: "He made us unto Himself an assembled people."

2:13 **And again: "I will put My trust in Him." And again: "Here am I and the children whom God has given Me."** This reiterates the notion that we are all one family in Christ (see previous verse).

2:14 **Inasmuch then as the children have partaken of flesh and blood, He Himself likewise shared in the same, that through death He might destroy him who had the power of death, that is, the devil.** We are flesh and blood, and the divine Lord Jesus Christ was willing to take flesh and blood to Himself and share in our humanity by becoming a man (incarnation). It was fitting for Christ to be incarnate, in order to identify with us in this way. Christ shared in another aspect of our humanity—the fact that humans die. God cannot die, but by becoming man, He was able to die, and through this death, Christ was able overcome death for all mankind. Christ, who shared our flesh and blood, and also our death, if He trampled over death, then through Christ we can also overcome death. Death is the wage of sin, so the restoration of our fallen humanity requires victory over death.

him who had the power of death, that is, the devil. Satan brought sin to the human race (Gen. 3:1-7), the result of which is death (Gen. 2:17; Rom. 6:23; Wisdom of Solomon 2:24). Satan is certainly behind the persecution and martyrdom of all Christians (Luke 12:4-5; Rev. 13:7), and that is why the Lord Christ called him *"a murderer from the beginning"* (John 8:44). Here, St. Paul says that the devil has power over death. Christ did not only trample upon death, but he also destroyed Satan who has the power over death.

✝ St. Athanasius ✝

Remarks on Heb. 2:9, 14

He [St. Paul] means that the rescue of mankind from corruption was the proper part only of Him who made them in the beginning. He points out also that the Word assumed a human body, expressly in order that He might offer it in sacrifice for other like bodies. . . . For by the sacrifice of His own body He did two things: He put an end to the law of death which barred our way; and He made a new beginning of life for us, by giving us the hope of resurrection. . . . Now, therefore, when we die we no longer do so as men condemned to death, but as those who are even now in process of rising we await the general resurrection of all, "which He will manifest in His own time" (1 Tim. 6. 15), even God Who wrought it and bestowed it on us.

- On the Incarnation of the Word, § 10

2:15 and release those who through fear of death were all their lifetime subject to bondage. St. Paul delineated (in the previous verse) the first of two purposes of Christ's death, the first being that His death overcame the devil. Here, St. Paul explains a second purpose of Christ's death, which is to free us from our bondage to the fear of death. Being sinful, we were made subject to death, and fearing death, we became in bondage to this fear. We were captives of an evil tyrant who possessed the power to intimidate us. When Christ came and shared in our flesh and blood through His death, He released us from the bondage of our fear of death. Now we do not fear death, as St. Paul says, *"to live is Christ, and to die is gain"* (Phil. 1:21). Christians should not fear death.

2:16 For indeed He does not give aid to angels, but He does give aid to the seed of Abraham. Christ shared in our flesh and blood because He came to help (*"give aid to"*) human beings, not angels (who are spirits, not flesh and blood like us).

2:17 Therefore, in all things He had to be made like His brethren. Christ resembled us in everything except sin only (as we say in the Liturgy of St. Gregory: "but You, without change, were incarnate and became man and resembled us in everything, except for sin alone." *"For He made Him who knew no sin to be sin for us, that we might become the righteousness of God in Him"* (2Cor. 5:21); *"Who committed no sin, nor was deceit found in His mouth"* (1 Pet. 2:22); *"And you know that He was manifested to take away our sins, and in Him there is no sin"* (1 John 3:5).

that He might be a merciful and faithful High Priest in things pertaining to God. This is another reason Christ became like us. St. Paul will elaborate below about the aspect of the priesthood as it pertains to Christ later, but for now we have two very important descriptions: merciful and faithful. Christ is merciful because, having been a human being, we can more easily identify with Him and see His compassion for us, having suffered and felt our pain. Christ is faithful in all things pertaining to God, so we can trust Him and put our full confidence in Him, because He is God.

to make propitiation for the sins of the people. As a faithful High Priest, the Lord Jesus Christ can stand before God the Father and offer propitiation for our sins, reconciling us with the Father by His blood.

2:18 **For in that He Himself has suffered, being tempted, He is able to aid those who are tempted.** Christ is a merciful High Priest, having suffered and having been tempted so that He can share our human experience of suffering and feeling pain. Christ was tempted like a human, yet knew no sin (see 2:17). He is merciful in subjecting Himself to sin and suffering, and in experiencing this He exhibits mercy to others who also experience the same. The remembrance of His own sorrows and temptations makes Him mindful of the trials of His people, and thus, always ready to help them. Note that the High Priest (like any priest in general) stands before God on behalf of the people, interceding on their behalf. Christ was a perfect High Priest, being merciful to the extent of sharing in our pains and temptations (feeling for our needs), yet, was also faithful by refraining from all sin and offering a satisfactory propitiation for our sins.

Chapter 2 Questions

1. How do we avoid drifting away?
2. Suffering is the way of glory. What does this mean to you?
3. What is your perception of death?
4. What should we do when we are tempted?

3

Chapter Outline

- Jesus is greater than Moses (1-6)
- Danger of unbelief: hardening of the heart (4-14)
- Keep from being hardened by sin's deceitfulness (12-14)
- Unbelief made it impossible to enter God's rest (15-19)

Introduction

The Hebrews were tempted to return back to Judaism. In Chapter 3, St. Paul is exhorting them to be faithful to Christ, and also to resist the rebelliousness that was shown by their ancestors. To convince them that they should not return to Judaism, St. Paul attempts to convince them that Christ is superior to Moses. When speaking about Moses, there is understood to be a connection between the law of Moses and angels, because the law is said to be given to Moses through angels (see commentary above on Heb. 2:2-4). Therefore, the first chapter focused on how Christ is superior to the angels who delivered the law. In this chapter, St. Paul reflects on how Christ is also superior to Moses. It was important for St. Paul to convince the Jews of this because of the status that Moses had in their eyes: the great leader to Israel, regarded as the founder of the Israelite faith and the Jewish religion.

St. Paul begins where he left off in Chapter 2. There he introduced the concept of Christ as the High Priest who has to possess two characteristics: faithfulness and mercifulness. Here he begins by focusing on the faithfulness of Christ, our High Priest.

3:1 holy brethren. St. Paul uses the word *"holy"* to remind them that Christians are called to be holy. In the Divine Liturgy (of the Coptic Orthodox Church), we remind the congregation before they partake of the Divine Eucharist, "the Holies for the holy." The "Holies" refers to the divine body and blood, while "the holy" refers to us, indicating we should approach the body and blood of Christ in holiness.

partakers of the heavenly calling. St. Paul reminds them that they are partakers of the inheritance of Christ, called to inherit the kingdom of heaven with Christ. *"If children, then heirs—heirs of God and joint heirs with Christ, if indeed we suffer with Him, that we may also be glorified together"* (Rom. 8:17); *"... fellow heirs, of the same body, and partakers of His promise in Christ through the gospel"* (Eph. 3:6); *"that having been justified by His grace we should become heirs according to the hope of eternal life"* (Titus 3:7).

consider. The word *"consider"* means to be engaged in serious thinking.

Why is St. Paul asking them to think seriously? The biblical writers are never interested in thinking that does not lead to action, but are interested in thinking that will transform our lives. As St. Paul said elsewhere, *"be transformed by the renewing of your mind"* (Rom. 12:2). So when we have correct thinking, and a mind that is renewed, we will be transformed and our lives will be changed. That is why he is telling them, I want you to be engaged in serous thinking—to consider having a right and sound doctrine because when you have the right thinking and correct thoughts, this will transform your life. Thoughts must transform your life. Thinking must change your actions. Correct living requires correct thinking about Christ. That is why St. Paul is trying to correct their image of Christ; when you have a correct image of Christ, this will transform your life.

the Apostle and High Priest of our confession, Christ Jesus. Now Christ is called Apostle and High Priest of our faith (our confession). What does this mean? Apostle refers to the one who is sent by the Father in order to fulfill a mission. Apostle means messenger, so the word here in this context means the one who is sent by the Father in order to fulfill the mission. What was the mission? It was the mission of priesthood, to offer Himself as a sacrifice for the salvation of the world. Not only was Christ a priest, but He also became the Altar and the Sacrifice, as St. Cyril of Alexandria is known to have said.

3:2 who was faithful to Him who appointed Him, as Moses also was faithful in all His house. This is the introduction St. Paul used to compare between Moses and Christ, how both of them were faithful in God's household (church). Moses was a steward in God's household, and Christ was a son. St. Paul will now begin to reflect on the faithfulness of Christ as the High Priest, saying that Christ was faithful to the Father, who appointed the Son (who sent the Son), just as Moses also was faithful in God's house after he was appointed to serve it. Faithfulness is therefore the common factor shared between the two.

3:3-4 For this One has been counted worthy of more glory than Moses, inasmuch as He who built the house has more honor than the house. For every house is built by someone, but He who built all things is God. In spite of the fact that Moses and Christ were both deemed faithful, Christ is counted worthy of more glory than Moses. He gave three reasons for this: First, Jesus, as the Son, who was described as the creator and builder in Chapter 1, is greater than Moses who was His creation. The builder is more honorable than the object which he built. Christ here is likened to a builder of a house, and the house He built is likened to Moses.

3:5-6 And Moses indeed was faithful in all His house as a servant, for a testimony of those things which would be spoken afterward, but Christ as a Son over His own house. The second reason Christ is worthy of more glory than Moses is that Moses acted as a servant over the household of God, while Jesus is the Son—true God of true God, begotten not created, light of light. Third, the honor given Moses is due to his faithfulness in relaying things that would eventually come to pass: promises that would be fulfilled, and testimony that would happen afterword. But Christ is the fulfillment of those promises. The fulfillment is obviously greater than the one who promises its fulfillment. Moses promised that salvation would come, whereas Christ fulfilled this promise because He is our savior.

whose house we are if we hold fast the confidence and the rejoicing of the hope firm to the end. We are His house, the Church of God, the assembly of believers. Before baptism, we are individuals, but afterward, we become members of this Church of believers. *"For as the body is one and has many members, but all the members of that one body, being many, are one body, so also is Christ. For by one Spirit we were all baptized into one body ... For in fact the body is not one member but many"* (1Cor. 12:12-14). St. Paul warns the Jewish Christians, being tempted to return back to their former Judaic religion, that they cannot be considered part of Christ's body unless they continue firmly in their faith as Christians. St. Paul used here four words that are essential for us to be considered the house of God. We are God's *"house" "if we hold fast"* the following four conditions: (1) Confidence—this is a state of courage, boldness, and fearlessness. We have to be confident that Christ is the only way to heaven. Our Confidence remains in Him, who is unchangeable, and for that reason, we can depend on Him because He is reliable. We are confident and proud that our way is the true way. This hope is not shaken, and should be retained until the Coming of Christ. Whatever pressures or difficulties we face everyday, Christ's faithfulness and His victory over Satan (who previously held the power of death—see Heb. 2:14) provides us with confidence and assurance that He is capable of meeting our needs also. (2) Hope—this refers to looking forward to something, expecting fulfillment of some future promise. Christ promised us eternal life, which is a hope in which we must be confident. (3) Rejoicing—this refers to taking pride in something. We should take pride in our faith, in following Christ, and that we are Christians. (4) Firm—we must adhere firmly to the doctrines, traditions, and beliefs of Christ's Church without drifting away.

3:7-11 St. Paul begins here to discuss the second of five warnings that he lays out in his Epistle to the Hebrews (see commentary on Heb. 2:1). In Chapter 2, the first warning—about the danger of neglect—was discussed. Here, we learn about the warning related to the danger of unbelief. In the previous verse (Heb. 3:6), we are introduced to the notion that we must remain faithful to the very end in order to remain members of Christ's Church. To prove this point, St. Paul recalls the story of when the Israelites fled from Egypt and were en route to the Promised Land. Specifically, he reminds us that when the Israelites did not hold firm to their confidence in God, they were not allowed to enter into the Promised Land, losing their status as being members of the household of God. Similarly, if the Jews returned to their former faith, or if we today turn our backs on the faith that we have received, we will also lose our chance at salvation in the Promised Land we seek to enter—eternal life in heaven with Christ.

Introductory remarks regarding Psalm 95, as quoted in Heb. 3:7-11:

In Psalm 95, we see a reflection on what the Israelites witnessed during the Exodus out of the land of Egypt. When there was no food, God provided manna. When there was no water, God gushed forth water from a rock: at Massah and Meribah (Ex. 17:7). But the crucial test occurred just before they were about to enter into the promised land (which can be read more fully in Numbers Chapters 13 and 14). Moses sent twelve persons to spy out the land of Canaan. When they returned, ten of them reported their impression that, although the land is beautiful, the Israelites would not be able to stand up against the walled cities and giants of the land. Only two people—Caleb and Joshua—returned expressing their faith in God that by Him the Israelites could defeat the Canaanites. *"Then Caleb quieted the people before Moses, and said, 'Let us go up at once and take possession, for we are well able to overcome it'"* (Num. 13:30). Their hope and confidence in God was firm unto the end. But what happened? Most of the people of Israel rebelled against God, following the advice of the ten rather than the two, due to their fear after hearing their report. Confidence involves a sense of fearlessness (see commentary on Heb. 3:5-6 for more). So this fear that these Israelites exhibited is contrary to confidence. There was even talk among the Israelites to select another leader in order to return back to Egypt—which is akin to apostasy. This was not rebellion against Moses as much as it was a lack of trust and confidence in God. King David refers to this is as *"rebellion"* (Heb. 3:8). God's response was very stern: *"but truly, as I live, all the earth shall be filled with the glory of the LORD— because all these men who have seen My glory and the signs which I did in Egypt and in the wilderness, and have put Me to the test now these ten times, and have not heeded My voice, they certainly shall not see the land of which I swore to their fathers, nor shall any of those who rejected Me see it"* (Num. 14:21-23). No man or woman who was twenty or older would enter into the land of promise. All of these people died in the land of Sinai. Only their children entered the land. The reason for this was because these older people would not have continued in faith toward God, having shown their lack of confidence and trust in Him. St. Paul, therefore, warns us here: if you want to be regarded as a member of the household of Christ, then you must hold fast, to the end, in the confidence and rejoicing of hope. But if you are going to be like the Israelites and commit apostasy as they did, then you will not be counted among the household of God. This was the same temptation with which the Jewish Christian leaders targeted by this Epistle struggled.

Therefore as the Holy Spirit. This is taken from Psalm 95. I want you to notice something. St. Paul did not say, "as David said," but rather regards the inspiration of this, and all Scripture, as being by the Holy Spirit—God Himself. Hence, it is not David, not Paul, nor Peter; rather, it is the Holy Spirit.

says. Moreover, St. Paul does not say here "as the Holy Spirit inspired David." He simply writes: *"as the Holy Spirit says."* The word *"says"* denotes a present reality, written in the present tense rather than in the past tense. The writings by David were not simply inspired once and left for us so that we may read a once inspired writing. The Holy Spirit did not inspire the writers of the Scriptures only, but the word *"says"* exemplifies how the Holy Spirit still continues to speak to each of us today when we read or hear the Scriptures. Therefore, the function of the Holy Spirit did not finish when He inspired the authors of the Scriptures, but the Holy Spirit continues to speak directly to us today. That is why we are told by St. Paul in Heb. 2:1 that *"we must give the more earnest heed to the things we have heard, lest we drift away."* The Bible has the power of the Holy Spirit, which is the anchor that will help keep us from drifting away.

Today, if you will hear His voice, do not harden your hearts as in the rebellion. The Hebrew word translated as *"hear"* and *"obey"* are one and the same. The Psalmist was not simply referring to hearing God's word, but also obeying it. This means having one's heart open and responsive toward His words, rather than being closed and hardened. St. Paul implores the Hebrews, who were being tempted away from Christianity to return back to Judaism, not to harden their hearts as the children of Israel did against God's efforts to strengthen and encourage them. This is applicable to us today, who face pressures and troubles from the world around us—but we must remain steadfast in our faith, confidence, and trust in Him. (Recall how God condemned the Israelites for not heeding His words spoken through His prophet Ezekiel: *"So they come to you as people do, they sit before you as My people, and they hear your words, but they do not do them; for with their mouth they show much love, but their hearts pursue their own gain. Indeed you are to them as a very lovely song of one who has a pleasant voice and can play well on an instrument; for they hear your words, but they do not do them"*—Ezek. 33:31-32).

In the day of trial in the wilderness, where your fathers tested Me, tried Me, And saw My works forty years. Who is trying whom? It is us testing God. We are the ones who test or try God. More clearly, it means we often demand that God prove Himself to us. This is the opposite of trust and obedience. When you have already fully committed to trusting another person, you do not continually remind the person that they need to prove themselves to you, telling them "you need to earn my trust." Doing this with God is contrary to faith and true confidence in Him.

Therefore I was angry with that generation, and said, "They always go astray in their heart, and they have not known My ways." What is the reason the Israelites go astray, such as in the time they sought to return to Egypt after God had just saved them from Pharaoh, or as in this instance about which St. Paul is writing pertaining to their inclination to return back to Judaism? It is because *"they have not known My ways."* If we know the way of God, we will be more capable of maintaining our journey and reaching its intended end.

So I swore in My wrath, "They shall not enter My rest." The word *"rest"* here is used to exemplify four meanings: either rest in the wilderness of Sinai, rest in the salvation of the Lord Jesus Christ, rest in the sense of God's rest in His creation as explained in Genesis (see Gen. 2:2-3), or as is meant here, eternal life, which is a beautiful way of conceptualizing the word *"rest"* (for more on these four meanings, see the commentary on Hebrews Chapter 4). God rested at the end of His creation. If you refuse to trust God and continue to harden your heart, you will be stuck in the process of creation; that is, God rested on the seventh day, a day (or state of creation) in which we are *"stuck,"* continually awaiting and looking forward to the eighth day in which we will live in a new heaven and earth, with new bodies, and in a completely new existence (see 1 Cor. 15:52; Is. 65:17, 22; 2 Pet. 3:13; Rev. 21:1). Thus, not entering into God's *"rest"* can refer to not reaching the goal of God's work in your life, due to a lack of trust in Him. In this way you will be incomplete, immature, and unfulfilled.

3:12 Beware, brethren, lest there be in any of you an evil heart of unbelief in departing from the living God. Then in verse 12, St. Paul gives us a warning against *"departing from the living God"*—apostasy. St. Paul describes apostasy as someone who has both an evil and unbelieving heart. An evil heart refers to those whose hearts are filled with vices rather than virtues. A person with an unbelieving heart is unwilling to commit himself or herself to God's hand. St. Paul is diagnosing the reason of apostasy as being due to one or both of these reasons: an evil heart, or an unbelieving one. Notice that the problem that many encounter—turning back on God, giving up on Him—is not because of persecution, or pressure, or the circumstances around us, but rather the problem is with our hearts. Many times we hear about people who depart from Christianity due to the pressure on them (such as peer pressure). The reason behind it was the heart, not the pressure. This is reminiscent of the words of St. Peter to the Lord Jesus Christ, telling Him *"Lord, to whom shall we go? You have the words of eternal life"* (John 6:68). When the heart is not evil but rather pure and is confident in Christ, then we will never turn away from Him, but instead say with St. Peter the same words: *"Lord, to whom shall we go? You have the words of eternal life."*

3:13 but exhort one another daily, while it is called "Today," lest any of you be hardened through the deceitfulness of sin. St. Paul gives us a remedy against the deceitfulness of sin and the hardness of one's heart. St. Paul inquires into how a person acquires an evil, hardened heart: it begins when sin hides in one's heart, remaining there until it becomes a constant presence. Sin is deceiving (as we say in the Divine Liturgy of the Coptic Church, according to St. Basil: "and when he fell by the deception of the Serpent"). Our fellowship with one another helps remedy the deceitfulness of sin. God called you to be a member in the family of God. Before baptism, you were individuals; but afterwards, you are not individuals—you are a member, part of the whole. The whole is the body of Christ. So now you are called to be a member in the family of Christ. In the Divine Liturgy according to St. Basil, the priest prays: "and He made us unto Himself an assembled people." He made us to assemble into His body, to be members in His body. We have a responsibility to one another to exhort (encourage or urge) one another every day. How can we expect not to fall into sin if we do not remain partakers of this household? Some succumb to deceitful thoughts such as, "no, I do not want to be a member of the Church, I would rather worship God by myself." St. Paul says we must remain in contact with each of the members of the household of God, continuing to exhort one another on a daily basis.

Today. We need encouragement every day to survive the pressures around us. We have a responsibility to support and encourage one another on a daily basis. Failure to encourage one another on a daily basis can lead to hardened hearts through the deceitfulness of sin.

Deceitfulness of sin. The power of Satan lies in his ability to deceive. St. Paul recognizes that Satan is deceitful. This word—deceitful—carries with it the notion of seductiveness. Sin many times seems pleasurable, but it is deadly.

3:14-15 **For we have become partakers of Christ if we hold the beginning of our confidence steadfast to the end, while it is said: "Today, if you will hear His voice, do not harden your hearts as in the rebellion."** This refers to Christians, who are sharers in the promise of the coming world—eternal life. St. Paul puts a condition here, which is the same as he mentioned before (Heb. 3:6): *"if we hold the beginning of our confidence steadfast to the end."* Participating in the world to come requires us to hold on to the confidence we have in Christ (which we started with) and remain steadfast in that confidence to the end, refraining from hardening our hearts as the Israelites did when they rebelled against God (See also commentary on Heb. 3:8-11).

3:16-19 **For who, having heard, rebelled? Indeed, was it not all who came out of Egypt, led by Moses? Now with whom was He angry forty years? Was it not with those who sinned, whose corpses fell in the wilderness? And to whom did He swear that they would not enter His rest, but to those who did not obey? So we see that they could not enter in because of unbelief.** St. Paul here begins to pose a series of three questions (taken ultimately from Psalm 95) and three answers (taken ultimately from Numbers Chapter 14). These questions and answers are relayed in the table below. St. Paul asks these three questions to make the audience of his letter think: those who came out of Egypt were taken from there in order to allow them to enter into the promised land, but instead of that, they wandered in the wilderness for forty years and were not permitted to enter into the land of Canaan, because they rebelled (v.16), sinned (v.17), and did not obey (v.18). These three words describe in totality one action—unbelief (v.19). Their unbelief was exhibited in their rebellion against God, sinning, and failing to obey Him. Likewise, if we are to exhibit characteristics amounting to unbelief, such as failing to maintain trust in God in the midst of persecution and pressure around us, then we too will be prohibited from entering the promised land (inheriting eternal life) and being partakers of Christ.

UNBELIEF MADE IT IMPOSSIBLE TO ENTER GOD'S REST (v.19)	
Questions taken from Psalm 95	**Answers taken from Numbers 14**
Who, having heard, rebelled? (Heb. 3:16; Ps. 95:7-8)	All who came out of Egypt, led by Moses. (Num. 14:13, 19, 22)
With whom was God angry for forty years? (Heb. 3:17; Ps. 95:10)	Those who sinned, whose corpses fell in the wilderness. (Num. 14:10, 29, 32)
To whom did He swear that they would not enter His rest? (Heb. 3:18; Ps. 95:11)	Those who did not obey. (Num. 14:30, 33, 43)

Chapter 3 Questions

1. Why is St. Paul exhorting his readers to "hold on" to Christ? What happens if we don't?

2. How does sin trick us? How does it harden us?

3. What is the value of Christian fellowship?

4

Chapter Outline

- Be sure to enter the promised rest (1-11)
- The living, powerful word of God (12-13)
- Our sympathetic High Priest (14-16)

Introduction

The theme of this epistle is to work against apostasy, to encourage the Jews not to return back to Judaism. He began comparing Christ with the angels, and then he spoke about Christ and Moses and proved the superiority of Christ over both angels and Moses. He also warned them regarding neglect—that they need to be careful about that which may return them back to Judaism.

At the end of the Chapter 3, St. Paul said that the sin of unbelief prevented the Israelites from entering the promised land. "And to whom did He swear that they would not enter His rest, but to those who did not obey? So we see that they could not enter in because of unbelief. (Heb. 3:18-19). The word "rest" can be understood in four different ways: the promised land, the Sabbath (the seventh day in which the Lord rested from His work as creator), salvation, and also eternal life. St. Paul will begin to establish here that through unbelief we will also be prevented from entering God's "rest"; whereas before, the Jews were kept from entering the promised land, but now, their unbelief (returning back to Judaism from their newfound Christian faith) will cause them to lose eternal life.

4:1 Therefore, since a promise remains of entering His rest, let us fear lest any of you seem to have come short of it. God's *"rest"* does not simply refer to the Sabbath day, otherwise, why would God speak of another *"rest"* as He did in the Book of Psalms and also as is referred to here by St. Paul. St. Paul says that the *"promise remains of entering His rest."* The Jews had already entered the promised land and were living in it. But this *"promise remains"* because they are still looking forward to another sort of "rest"— eternal life. The "Promised Land" is a type (or foreshadowing) of the spiritual rest in the heavenly Promised Land. St. Paul is telling us that we should be very careful to ensure we do not miss out on entering the "rest" of God—heaven.

4:2 For indeed the gospel was preached to us as well as to them; but the word which they heard did not profit them, not being mixed with faith in those who heard it. The *"gospel"* refers to the "good news" about Christ and His salvation. This does not refer specifically to the four books in the New Testament referred to as the Gospels, attributed to Saints Matthew, Mark, Luke, and John. This good news of entering God's rest (heaven) was preached to Christians as it was preached to the Israelites: that it was God's promise to let them dwell in the earthly promised land. But the word of promise did not profit them. Nowadays in the era of Christianity, merely hearing about what God has promised through Christ is not enough to obtain that promise. Simply hearing the word of promise did not profit the Jews because it was not *"mixed with faith in those who heard it."* St. Paul is referring to the rebellion of the Israelites (as explained in the commentary above on Heb. 3:7-11—see "Introductory remarks regarding Psalm 95"). Hearing the message, alone, does not save a person. Rather, this hearing should be combined with faith in this message. Because of the unbelief of the Israelites, everyone died without entering the Promised Land except for two people. The *"faith"* needed now means we must translate our belief into action: we must obey God's commandments, repent, and act on the promise God has made. That is why St. James says, *"be doers of the word, and not hearers only"* (James 1:22).

belief into action (see commentary on previous verse), then we will certainly enter His rest, inheriting the Kingdom of God.

as He has said: "So I swore in My wrath, 'They shall not enter My rest,' " although the works were finished from the foundation of the world. God prohibited them from entering His rest because of their unbelief; on the other hand God will grant the believers access to the Kingdom of Heaven. As it was sure and certain that those who did not believe in God's promise in the past did not enter into the Promised Land, so too it is now sure and certain that those who believe will inherit God's eternal, heavenly rest.

although the works were finished from the foundation of the world. In understanding which of the four definitions of *"rest"* apply here (see Introduction of this chapter for more information), St. Paul is making clear that the Sabbath is not what is referred to here. When God said *"My rest,"* He was not referring to God's *"rest"* on the seventh day—the Sabbath. This is instead a metaphorical reference to eternal life.

4:3 For we who have believed do enter that rest. St. Paul is emphasizing that, if we believe in God's promise about eternal life and translate that

4:4-5 For He has spoken in a certain place of the seventh day in this way: "And God rested on the seventh day from all His works"; and again in this place: "They shall not enter My rest. St. Paul grounds the certainty of the existence and the reality of rest (in heaven) on the foundation of two things that cannot contradict: God's action, and God's word. Regarding His action, He has been *"resting"* since the completion of His work of creation (Genesis 2:2), which is the seventh day (Sabbath) in which we are now living. Yet, God gave us His word that the Israelites who rebelled *"shall not enter My rest."* In order to harmonize these two things, St. Paul asks us to join in his conclusion that, since all humans live in what is called God's *"rest"*—(the seventh day), the *"rest"* of which God speaks here, no one was experiencing it, because it is different than the Sabbath. The Israelites referred to here were living during the era referred to as the seventh day—the day (which is not simply 24 hours but the era of human existence) in which God rested from His work of creation, which we live in now; therefore, they can be said to have been living during the era of God's "rest." Yet God says the Israelites *"shall not enter My rest."* To make these two statements make sense, St. Paul is telling us that this second use of the word "rest" is a reference to eternal life.

4:6-9 Since therefore it remains that some must enter it, and those to whom it was first preached did not enter because of disobedience, again He designates a certain day, saying in David, "Today," after such a long time, as it has been said: "Today, if you will hear His voice, Do not harden your hearts." For if Joshua had given them rest, then He would not afterward have spoken of another day. There remains therefore a rest for the people of God. God's "rest" to which we have access through Christ's saving death and resurrection is a continuing and present reality, in which we live here through salvation and which we are granted access to enjoy eternally. As explained in the commentary on the previous verse, when God said to the Israelites that they will not enter into God's "rest" because of their disobedience, yet God speaks of another day on which we will be allowed to enter some sort of "rest," then we understand that God is telling us that we have access to another sort of "rest" other than the Promised Land, which is eternal life. If David said "Today" you will enter God's rest, that means no one has experience it yet. King David wrote this many years after Joshua and the Israelites inhabited the Promised Land; thus, this "rest" which God says they may receive if they do not harden their hearts does not refer to the Promised Land, but rather to what the earthly Promised Land foreshadows: eternal life. The eventual entry of the Israelites into the Promised Land under the leadership of Joshua is not to be considered the real rest of God's people. It is only a prophetic physical shadow of the real Sabbath rest which is still available for God's people. The conclusion, after reading these verses and making sense of them all, is that there still "remains therefore a rest for the people of God"—eternal rest in heaven. We can say that the true rest is our Lord Jesus Christ. We will be comforted in Him when we accept Him, believe in Him, obey Him, and follow in His manner of life. We will find rest here and also in the afterlife. While four definitions for the term *"rest"* have been provided previously, we can add a fifth: Christ, our true and ultimate rest. Christ promises us rest in Him: *"Come to Me, all you who labor and are heavy laden, and I will give you rest. Take My yoke upon you and learn from Me, for I am gentle and lowly in heart, and you will find rest for your souls"* (Matt. 11:28-29). The Lord Jesus Christ is the fulfillment of the antitype to which the weekly Sabbaths pointed. In Him, we as believers will live in a perpetual, spiritual rest.

4:10 For he who has entered His rest has himself also ceased from his works as God did from His. Now St. Paul makes a comparison between the seventh day in which God rested form His work in creation, and the rest that we will enjoy when we believe in God and inherit His Kingdom. St. Paul tells us, when we enter the rest of God, we will rest from our own works. To understand what he means, let us refer to what St. John said in Revelations 14:13: *"Then I heard a voice from heaven saying to me, 'Write: "Blessed are the dead who die in the Lord from now on."' 'Yes,' says the Spirit, 'that they may rest from their labors, and their works follow them.'"* As the Lord rested from His work on the seventh day, our day of rest (like God's Sabbath in which He rests) is when we enter into heaven. There, God will wipe all our tears and be our comfort. *"For the Lamb who is in the midst of the throne will shepherd them and lead them to living fountains of waters. And God will wipe away every tear from their eyes"* (Rev. 7:17); *"And God will wipe away every tear from their eyes; there shall be no more death, nor sorrow, nor crying. There shall be no more pain, for the former things have passed away"* (Rev. 21:4).

4:11 Let us therefore be diligent to enter that rest, lest anyone fall according to the same example of disobedience. St. Paul used the word disobedience as synonymous to the word unbelief. We have to believe the good news that the Kingdom of God is our inheritance, and the promise of His Kingdom should motivate us to strive daily for God. If you promise a student in college that they will receive a certain job if they finish their education, when the student is confident in the certainty of the actualization of this promise, it is expected the student will make every effort to obtain that promise. In like manner, our promise of rest in Christ and eternal life will encourage us daily to remain *"diligent to enter the rest"* of God.

4:12 **For the word of God is living and powerful, and sharper than any two-edged sword, piercing even to the division of soul and spirit, and of joints and marrow, and is a discerner of the thoughts and intents of the heart.** If ignoring and rebelling against the words of God kept the Israelites out of the Promised Land, we must take God's words seriously— both words of promise and words of punishment. Understanding it in this way, we can understand how, beginning with this verse, St. Paul switches from speaking about God's rest to speaking about the word of God. Your first impression may be that there is a break in the flow of this passage, speaking about God's rest and then suddenly speaking about the word of God. We can understand the logic behind this as follows: St. Paul tells us that the word of God was not taken seriously by the Israelites, neglecting it and failing to believe it, and that is why they did not enter into the Promised Land. That is why we need to take the word of God seriously. Now, he introduces to us what the word of God is. (Recall that the word of God can mean what is in the Bible; the Word of God is also Christ Himself—the Logos.) In verse 12-13, St. Paul is telling us that the word of God has a way of uncovering our weaknesses and also our tendencies to go astray. The word of God will not only reveal our external actions, but also the motivations and intentions of our hearts.

living and powerful. *"Living"* means that the word of God is alive, and also capable of giving life to others. *"Powerful,"* in the Greek language, shares the same root as the word "energy." Thus, one can deduce that this describes something capable, effective, and active. When the word of God enters my heart, because it is energetic, it is capable of giving me life, piercing my heart, and transforming my life. We can see this on the day of Pentecost. St. Peter, who shortly before this denied Christ three times out of fear, all of a sudden is found preaching to thousands of people. When the people heard the word of God through St. Peter, *"they were cut to the heart"* (Acts 2:37); that is the action of the word of God, which is living and powerful. At this time we may recall Isaiah 55:11, where God declares that His word which He sends out will not return to Him empty or void, but will accomplish the goal for which it was spoken. (*"So shall My word be that goes forth from My mouth; it shall not return to Me void, but it shall accomplish what I please, and it shall prosper in the thing for which I sent it."*)

sharper than any two-edged sword. When we think about any two-edged sword, it is powerful but it is also dangerous. One edge can help me fight Satan, while the other edge can cut through my ungodliness and cleanse me.

piercing even to the division of soul and spirit, and of joints and marrow. Is there a division between soul and spirit? Actually, we cannot separate the two from each other. However, when St. Paul says this, he wants to tell us that this word is powerful and effective—that it can even penetrate between undivided components. The soul is the seat of the inner life, but the spirit is the part of the human personality that contains the *"breath of life"* (Gen. 2:7) and relates to the Divine Spirit. (Recall that the Old Testament teaches us that "the blood is the life" of a person or animal [Deut. 12:23; see also Gen 9:4], while God's breath in us is distinctly a human characteristic, which is the Divine Spirit of God). The word of God is so powerful that it can separate the inseparable. In similar fashion, the joints and marrow, while virtually inseparable, are no match for the word of God.

discerner of the thoughts and intents of the heart. The word of God acts like a judge. Think of a mirror, when you look at it, you will see what aspects of your physical image needs to be addressed. In the same way, the words of God will serve as a mirror showing you the weaknesses in the external man as well as in the internal man. The word of God can discern what cannot be seen from the outside, such as the hidden thoughts and intentions of the heart. In the face of such discernment, we cannot escape.

4:13 And there is no creature hidden from His sight, but all things are naked and open to the eyes of Him to whom we must give account. We find St. Paul in this verse referring to Christ as being the Word of God. We can deceive anyone, even ourselves, but we cannot deceive God. For with God, nothing is hidden from Him. Before God, we are all naked and thus unprotected, laid bare before His searching eyes.

to whom we must give account. The words of God will judge us in the Last Day, as Christ told us, *"He who rejects Me, and does not receive My words, has that which judges him—the word that I have spoken will judge him in the last day"* (John 12:48). So the word that you read, hear, and the word that penetrates your heart will judge you on the day of accountability. Thus, we must receive the words of God with obedience, unlike the Israelites.

4:14 Seeing then that we have a great High Priest who has passed through the heavens, Jesus the Son of God, let us hold fast our confession. After St. Paul discusses God's rest and how it is important to obey the word of God to inherit the eternal rest, he returns to the subject of Christ as the High Priest. St. Paul already mentioned (beginning in Chapter 2, then mostly in Chapter 3) two characteristics of a High Priest; that he is supposed to be both faithful and merciful. St. Paul transitions from the previous verses to this subject by concluding with verse 13, speaking about our having to give account before God. This may make some of us afraid, so St. Paul tells us that, yes, while we are accountable, we have a High Priest who is most merciful, sharing in our humanity having become man, understanding our weaknesses and our temptations, so that as The High Priest, He can intercede for us. For this reason, we should remain confident, strong, and *"hold fast our confession."*

High Priest who has passed through the heavens. The High Priest used to enter the Holy of the Holies once a year. But our Lord Jesus Christ did not enter through the veil to the earthly holy of holies. Instead, Christ entered the heavens to the very presence of God Himself, sitting at the right Hand of His Father.

Jesus the Son of God, let us hold fast our confession. Jesus Christ, who is the Son of God, was also the Son of Man (a real human being). He is the human son of a human mother who walked in our dust, cried our tears, and bled our blood. He resembled us in everything but sin alone. That is why He is a merciful High Priest. But He is also more than this, being the divine Son of God. Therefore, since we have such a High Priest who is fully and perfectly qualified to represent us as a man in the presence of God, yet at the same time is the exalted divine Son of God who came down to earth specifically to accomplish this for us, *"let us hold fast our confession."* No one could be more committed to our good than our Lord Jesus Christ. Remember that Satan tried deceiving Eve by telling her that he was more interested in benefiting humanity than God: *"You will not surely die. For God knows that in the day you eat of it your eyes will be opened, and you will be like God, knowing good and evil"* (Gen. 3:4-5). However, this is obviously not true, because you will find no one more committed to us than Christ. Moreover, you will never find someone more qualified or be better equipped to represent us in the presence of God, or be more capable of obtaining eternal salvation for us: "Neither an angel nor an archangel, neither a patriarch nor a prophet, have You entrusted with our salvation" as we say in the Liturgy of St. Basil. To ignore this High Priest, there is no other whom you can find to accomplish your need for salvation. To reject or turn aside from this provision of God is to make a final and absolute rejection of God, because there is no hope for salvation outside of Christ.

4:15 For we do not have a High Priest who cannot sympathize with our weaknesses, but was in all points tempted as we are, yet without sin. Our High Priest can sympathize with our weaknesses. How can we understand this perfect High Priest as having been tempted? This is possible because He took our humanity and lived among us experiencing our rejection and our hatred, hearing our false accusations, and feeling the pain of mocking thorns and nails. Christ did not only suffer physically, but He allowed Satan to tempt Him. We can find an example of explicit temptation in the gospels, when Christ went to the wilderness for forty days (Matt. 4, Mark 1, Luke 4); there, He was tempted more than just three times, but was *"tempted for forty days by the devil"* (Luke 4:2). It is important to understand here the distinction between being tempted and falling into temptation. We say in the Lord's Prayer, *"lead us not into temptation,"* which involves us asking that God not allow us to fall into temptation. Satan can tempt us, but we can reject this temptation. That is what happened with the Lord Jesus Christ. When confronted with temptation, Christ immediately countered these thoughts with correct ones. *"Away with you, Satan!"*—Matt. 4:10. He was pushed to the very limit of temptation's power by the great deceiver, until *"the devil left Him"* (Matt. 4:11). With such a High Priest, only one response is appropriate: absolute confidence.

4:16 Let us therefore come boldly to the throne of grace, that we may obtain mercy and find grace to help in time of need. Do not allow the throne of accountability make you scared, causing you to refrain from boldness and confidence to approach the throne of judgment. Many people are scared to participate in confession to a priest, having fear about their accountability. If that is why you are scared, do not focus on yourself, but rather think of the great High Priest who understands your weaknesses. Notice that St. Paul refers to God's place of judgment as the *"throne of grace"* rather than God's "judgment seat" or "throne of judgment." This is because God bore our sins instead of us, so that the throne of God that is indeed a throne of judgment, is now also a throne of grace if we follow in Christ's steps. We can obtain mercy (referring to God's recognition of our weaknesses, ineptness, need, and in response, He is doing whatever is necessary for our good and our survival) and also grace (the act of God in which He chooses to save us from sin and its consequences). In the absolution that the priest prays for the person who has confessed, we hear, "O Master who knows the weakness of men, as a Good One and Lover of Mankind, O God, grant us the forgiveness of our sins." We appeal to His familiarity with the weaknesses of our human condition.

Chapter 4 Questions

1. What do you think St. Paul meant by this promise of "rest" for the believers?

2. Why do we need to continually expose ourselves to the word of God?

3. What is so important about "holding fast to our confession"?

4. In what ways did the Lord Jesus share our weaknesses? In what ways was Jesus tempted?

5. Why should we approach the "throne of grace" with boldness and confidence?

1.

5

Chapter Outline

- The qualifications of the high priest (1-3)
- Christ's qualification as being the High Priest (5-10)
- The third warning: dullness of hearing (11-14)

Introduction

Starting with Chapter 5 and through to Chapter 10, St. Paul begins to contrast two things: Christ as the greatest High Priest and the high priests of the Jews; and the ritual animal sacrifices of the old covenant offered by the high priest as compared with the sacrifice of our Lord Jesus Christ. It is interesting to notice that the Lord Jesus Christ is the High Priest, the Sacrifice, and also, as St. Cyril is known to have said, He is the Altar. We will elaborate more on this matter later.

5:1-4. St. Paul mentions six qualifications for a high priest in these four verses.

5:1 taken from among men. The benefit of having a high priest selected from among other men is that he will be compassionate, because he himself also is subject to weakness, thus being able to identify with others. This also serves as a drawback, that the priest has to offer sacrifices for his own forgiveness as he also has to offer sacrifices for the people. Then, when St. Paul compares Christ, the ultimate High Priest, and the high priests of the Israelites, he will discuss how Christ lacks the need to offer sacrifices, being without blemish.

appointed for men in things pertaining to God. He is appointed to represent men in matters pertaining to God. The main function of the high priest is to intercede on behalf of his people, standing before God, offering sacrifices on their behalf. That is why he has to be faithful, so that he can stand before God. He also has to be compassionate and merciful, in order to intercede for the people. Samuel the prophet, who was also a priest, understood his function as a priest and said, *"Moreover, as for me, far be it from me that I should sin against the LORD in ceasing to pray for you"* (1 Sam. 12:23). He understood his role as a priest. Thus, as a priest, it would be a sin for him to cease praying for his people, as that is the main function of a priest. The main difference between a prophet and a priest is as follows: a prophet hears God and conveys the message to the people; the priest hears from the people and presents their supplications to God. Thus, the high priest is appointed for men in the following *"things pertaining to God"*:

presenting the prayers and requests of the people to God, and interceding on their behalf for their weaknesses before His throne.

that he may offer both gifts and sacrifices for sins. When you study the sacrifices in the book of Leviticus, you will find that the word *"sacrifice"* means a bloody offering (involving a shedding of blood; e.g., burnt offering, peace offering, sin offering, trespass offering). But there is another offering that does not involve the shedding of blood, like the grain offering (Leviticus 2). So when he says here *"gifts,"* he refers to the offerings that do not involve shedding of blood, while the term *"sacrifices"* refers to those that do.

5:2 He can have compassion on those who are ignorant and going astray, since he himself is also subject to weakness. Being subject to weakness, the priest is able to have compassion on his people, dealing gently with them. When we speak of the incarnation of Christ, it was absolutely necessary. For Christ to offer sacrifices on our behalf, He has to be the Son of Man, incarnated from among us, in order that He be compassionate with us. That is why you read in Chapter 4 the following: *"For we do not have a High Priest who cannot sympathize with our weaknesses, but was in all points tempted as we are, yet without sin"* (Heb. 4:15). That is why the incarnation of Christ was so important. Now with regard to the mention of the words *"ignorant"* and *"going astray,"* St. Paul is saying that Christ's compassion was directed toward those who sin unintentionally (by error or ignorance) and those who sinned presumptuously (arrogantly and acting intentionally against God). To understand this, let us turn to the Book of Numbers, Chapter 15, from verses 27 to 31, where you will find this differentiation of sin: *"And if a person sins unintentionally, then he shall bring a female goat in its first year as a sin offering. So the priest shall make atonement for the person who sins unintentionally, when he sins unintentionally before the LORD, to make atonement for him; and it shall be forgiven him. You shall have one law for him who sins unintentionally, for him who is native-born among the children of Israel and for the stranger who dwells among them. But the person who does anything presumptuously, whether he is native-born or a stranger, that one brings reproach on the LORD, and he shall be cut off from among his people. Because he has despised the word of the LORD, and has broken His commandment, that person shall be completely cut off; his guilt shall be upon him."* So it is clear in this passage how the Book of Numbers differentiates between those who sin out of weakness or ignorance, and those who sin out of arrogance and pride with an intention to resist God. In the Gregorian Liturgy we say, *"As true light, you shone upon the* *lost and the ignorant."* Also, in Luke 15, when the Lord spoke about the lost coin, the lost sheep, and the prodigal son, we notice that the woman went to search for the lost coin and the shepherd went to search for the lost sheep, both of which represent those who sinned due to weakness or other error in judgment; but in the case of the prodigal son, the father did not go and search for him, as he represents those who are lost due to their arrogance.

5:3 Because of this he is required as for the people, so also for himself, to offer sacrifices for sins. Being surrounded by weakness, so he is also sinful. That is why he has to offer sacrifices for himself as well as for all the people.

5:4 And no man takes this honor to himself, but he who is called by God, just as Aaron was. The last qualification of the high priest is that he has to be called and appointed by God. St. Paul was alluding to the well known story of Korah and Abiram who wanted to take the priesthood for themselves without being called by God (Num. 16). And what happened to them? *"The ground split apart under them, and the earth opened its mouth and swallowed them up, with their households and all the men with Korah, with all their goods. So they and all those with them went down alive into the pit; the earth closed over them, and they perished from among the assembly"* (Num. 16:31-33). And in the gospel of St. John, Christ tells the people, *"You did not choose Me, but I chose you and appointed you"* (John 15:16). The priesthood is a calling, not something men choose for themselves based on some personal whim or feeling.

5:5-10 Now St. Paul starts to compare between the high priesthood of Christ and the high priesthood of the Levites (the sons of Aaron). To better provide and understanding of this comparison, I will begin by referring to the previous chapter of this epistle.

The first difference between Christ and Aaron (and his sons) is from the following: "Seeing then that we have a great High Priest who has passed through the heavens, Jesus the Son of God, let us hold fast our confession" (Heb. 4:14). This is the first comparison. Aaron, as a high priest, goes through a veil, in order to enter the Holy of Holies. But Christ did not cross through a man-made curtain, but instead went through heaven, not to enter a man-made sanctuary, but instead went to the heaven of heavens.

As mentioned previously, Christ became the Son of Man so that we can identify ourselves better with Him, and we can truly believe that

He sympathizes with our weaknesses, having been tempted in every way, just as we are tempted. *"For we do not have a High Priest who cannot sympathize with our weaknesses, but was in all points tempted as we are, yet without sin"* (Heb. 4:15). The remaining points of comparison are provided below.

5:5-6 **So also Christ did not glorify Himself to become High Priest, but it was He who said to Him: "You are My Son, today I have begotten You." As He also says in another place: "You are a priest forever according to the order of Melchizedek."** As the high priest was appointed by God, so also Christ was appointed by God. He did not glorify Himself to become the High Priest, but it was the Father who said to Christ, *"You are My Son, today I have begotten You."* St. Paul is also saying, the hypostasis of the Father addressed the hypostasis of Christ, who was appointed to be a priest but not according to the order and lineage of Aaron, but rather according to the order of Melchizedek (see Genesis 14 for more information on this elusive persona in the Bible, who brought bread and wine to Abraham, and to whom Abraham offered tithes, although hardly anything about the background story of this "priest of God Most High" is told to us).

5:7 **who, in the days of His flesh, when He had offered up prayers and supplications, with vehement cries and tears to Him who was able to save Him from death.** St. Paul elaborates more on why Christ can sympathize with our weakness. Christ, by experiencing the suffering, agony, and temptations of man, is qualified to be regarded as a perfect representative for us. Now, the prayers and supplications to which St. Paul is referring is almost certainly those that were offered in the garden of Gethsemane. Christ prayed saying, *"'Father, if it is Your will, take this cup away from Me; nevertheless not My will, but Yours, be done.' Then an angel appeared to Him from heaven, strengthening Him. And being in agony, He prayed more earnestly. Then His sweat became like great drops of blood falling down to the ground"* (Luke 22:42-44). (St. Luke, as a physician [according to tradition], explained the agony of Christ in a very expressive way.)

and was heard. Now, many people may read the phrase indicating that Christ was *"heard because of His godly fear"* and wonder how that could be the case if Christ died on the cross. (Some may think Christ prayed for release from His plight). Actually, the Lord Jesus Christ, when He prayed in Gethsemane, He did not pray not to die or suffer on the cross. He made it clear that this was His purpose for becoming incarnate and living on earth among us: *"Now My soul is troubled, and what* *shall I say? 'Father, save Me from this hour?' But for this purpose I came to this hour"* (John 12:27). Pay close attention to Christ's request: *"Father, if it is Your will, take this cup away from Me."* He is saying, Father, if it is Your will and You want to do this, seeing it more fitting to take this cup from Me, I am fully aware of Your ability to do so. Instead of Christ being regarded as having shied away from His mission, this event rather exhibits Christ's trust in the Father's abilities to do as He pleases. This lack of doubt on Christ's part in the Father's abilities was expressed also when the Jews gathered around Christ to capture Him, at which time St. Peter responded by trying to draw a sword to defend his master, to which Christ responded: *"Do you think that I cannot now pray to My Father, and He will provide Me with more than twelve legions of angels?"* (Matt. 26:53). Christ prayed, *"Nevertheless not My will, but Yours, be done."* This does not indicate a conflict between the will of the Father and the will of the Son, because Their will is one (*"Believe Me that I am in the Father and the Father in Me"*—John 14:11). This shows, instead, the utter submission to the will of the Father. When St. Paul says Christ was *"heard,"* it is the prayer "not My will, but Yours" that was heard, and truly Christ was saved from death by His resurrection.

because of His godly fear. The term "godly fear" refers to Christ's complete submission to the will of the Father. Here St. Paul is sending a message to the Hebrews. Now you suffer, and there is pressure on you to return back to Judaism. I want you to do as Christ, who complied with the will of the Father, so also wholly surrender your will to the Father (as we say in the Lord's Prayer, *"Your will be done"* (Luke 11:2). And do not doubt that the Father can save you from the sufferings and persecutions in which you have now find found yourself in. This reminds me of those who, during moments of oppression and persecution of the church, ask, *"Where are You God? Why do You not attend to our prayers?"* That is not the appropriate remark, as it denies the fact that God is able to save us from every persecution, but if He allows us to suffer, this is for our own glory, because *"if indeed we suffer with Him"* then *"we may also be glorified together"* with Him (Rom. 8:17). In the following verses, St. Paul continues to discuss the way that suffering is the path to royal glory.

5:8 though He was a Son, yet He learned obedience by the things which He suffered. He was a Son, not by adoption, but by nature, being "Light of Light, and true God of true God" (as the Orthodox Creed indicates). Although He is the Son, He submitted His will completely to the Father, accepting suffering. That is why, if we are God's children, we should also accept suffering, carrying our cross and following the Lord Jesus Christ (*"Then He said to them all, 'If anyone desires to come after Me, let him deny himself, and take up his cross daily, and follow Me.'"*— Luke 9:23; *"And whoever does not bear his cross and come after Me cannot be My disciple."*—Luke 14:27).

learned obedience. This word *"learned"* means Christ fulfilled, practiced, and lived a life of obedience when He accepted to suffer on our behalf. You can substitute the word "fulfilled" or "exhibited" for the word learned.

5:9 And having been perfected. As explained previously in Chapter 2, this word "perfected" does not mean Christ was previously imperfect, but rather means that Christ fulfilled His mission, the goal for which He was incarnated. *"For by Him all things were created ... through Him and for Him."* How do we become perfect? These verses teach us that we need to obey through suffering and submitting to the will of God, allowing us to be perfect as Christ was perfect.

He became the author of eternal salvation to all who obey Him. As Christ obeyed the Father, then if we in turn obey Him. He will be the author (or source) of our eternal salvation. Just like the high priest in the Old Testament who offered gifts and sacrifices on behalf of the people for their forgiveness, likewise Christ is the source of salvation, bestowing it upon all who follow and abide by Him.

5:10 called by God as High Priest "according to the order of Melchizedek." Briefly, this is intended to relay the notion that Christ was not a High Priest according to the order of Aaron, but rather the order of Melchizedek. Because St. Paul elaborates about this in Chapter 7, I will reserve my discussion of this subject there.

5:11-14 As mentioned previously, the letter to the Hebrews contains five warnings. The first warning was the danger of neglect (Chapter 2), and the second warning was the danger of unbelief (Chapters 3 and 4). Here in Chapter 5, St. Paul relays to us the third warning, which is the danger of spiritual immaturity. What causes this? St. Paul says it is the due to dullness of hearing (the dullness of understanding).

5:11 of whom we have much to say, and hard to explain, since you have become dull of hearing. When there is a subject that is hard to explain, there are three reasons that this can happen: the material may be difficult, or the teacher may not be eloquent, or the students are not intelligent enough to grasp the information presented. Let us determine why St. Paul says that speaking about Christ is hard to explain to the Hebrews. First, is the material—the subject matter—too difficult to grasp? No, it is not. Second, is St. Paul not eloquent? Of course not, he is a great teacher and philosopher. The problem then is not in the first or the second, but rather the third reason for the difficulty in explaining about Christ: *"since you have become dull of hearing."* In the Jewish mind, the words hearing, obeying, and understanding are to some degree synonymous. St. Paul is telling them, therefore, it is not because you are unintelligent, or because you are not intellectuals, but it is because you refuse to obey. St. Paul wants to explain to them that obedience leads to understanding. Many times kids will come to us and say, explain why I should do this or that, and then I will be obedient to it. But there are many things that have to be performed and experienced in order to mentally grasp its benefit. For example, if before you receive an explanation as to its importance, you obey and pray, or you are obedient regarding the notion of confessing to a priest, or obey and begin to study the Bible, your experiences performing those tasks will inform you as to why they are beneficial. A lecture about prayer, Confession, or reading the Bible will not sufficiently motivate and provide an adequate explanation for why we do these things and their advantages. That is why Job said, *"I have heard of You by the hearing of the ear, but now my eye sees You"* (Job 42:5). Thus, when we demand understanding before obedience, we limit our spiritual growth. For example, if Abraham said to God, "Make me understand first why I should offer my son as a sacrifice to You," there would have been no way to adequately explain that. But nonetheless, he obeyed God, which obedience progressed his spiritual maturity. That is why when Christ was going to wash the feet of the disciples and St. Peter told Him, *"You shall never wash my feet,"* Christ responded by asking him to simply obey before understanding, *"What I am doing you do not understand now, but you will know after this"* (John 13:7). We obey, and then understand, not because it contradicts our reasoning, but because it is to some degree above reason.

5:12 For though by this time you ought to be teachers, you need someone to teach you again the first principles of the oracles of God; and you have come to need milk and not solid food. The disobedience of the Jews led to their spiritual infancy. St. Paul tells them that, since they have been Christians for so long, they ought to have by this point become teachers, but unfortunately, *"you need someone to teach you again the first principles of* *the oracles of God; and you have come to need milk and not solid food."*

5:13 For everyone who partakes only of milk is unskilled in the word of righteousness, for he is a babe. But solid food belongs to those who are of full age, that is, those who by reason of use have their senses exercised to discern both good and evil. Because the Jews whom St. Paul was addressing were spiritual infants, they exhibited a lack of appropriate discernment, being *"unskilled in the word of righteousness."* The skill spoken of here is the ability to discern. Being skilled in the *"word of righteousness,"* we will be able to make good choices. True believers are trained by obedience to distinguish between good and evil. St. Paul wants Christians to know how to make tough choices between eternal salvation and temporary comfort, and between painful obedience and the path of least resistance. Many times we do not want to carry our cross here, wanting to go through the wide gate rather than the narrow one. This is not a righteous decision, but if you are skilled in the *"word of righteousness"* you will know what choice is best.

reason of use. Christians develop spiritual understanding by the discipline of constant use: when you train yourself by constantly hearing the word of God and obeying it, you will develop the wisdom of discernment and understand the depth and grace of the word of God. Those of us who pray one week, and stop for many months, then pray again for a short period of time, and stop again for an extended amount of time, are not practicing this notion of constant use. St. Paul wants us to enhance our skills by *"the reason of use."*

senses exercised. Our senses are exercised through suffering. Recall Hebrews 5:8, when St. Paul said about Christ, *"yet He learned obedience by the things which He suffered."* Many people, upon confronting suffering, quit their attempts at spiritual progression. However, on the contrary, it is through these exercises of our senses through suffering (e.g., temptation, persecution, etc.) we will learn obedience to God.

discern both good and evil. When we train ourselves constantly, continually using our senses in a manner obedient to God's will irrespective of the suffering we endure, the sign of spiritual maturity will be the ability to distinguish between good and evil and make wise decisions.

Chapter 5 Questions

1. Analyze each of the high priests's qualifications (5:1-4) and identify in what ways the Lord Jesus is superior.

2. In what sense did the Lord Jesus "learn obedience from what He suffered"?

3. How does a person become mature in God's word according to verse 14? What can you do to grow in maturity?

6

Chapter Outline

- A call to perfection (1-3)
- Danger of apostasy (4-8)
- Encouragement to persevere (9-12)
- God's promise is steadfast (13-20)

Introduction

As Chapter 5 was concluding, St. Paul rebuked the Hebrews because of how sluggish they were in their understanding, being *"dull of hearing"* (Heb. 5:10), not reaching the spiritual stature they should have reached by this point. Thus, St. Paul tells them that, although by now they should have become so proficient in their understanding of Christianity that they should have been able to teach others, yet instead they needed to be reminded again about the Christian basics. *"For though by this time you ought to be teachers, you need someone to teach you again the first principles of the oracles of God"* (Heb. 5:12). In this Chapter, St. Paul addresses the need to be "laying again the foundation" of Christianity.

6:1-2 Therefore, leaving the discussion of the elementary principles of Christ. St. Paul wants to move away from the subject of the foundational tenets of Christianity, but before doing so, he feels the need to first give a brief rendition of what those *"elementary principles,"* are in the following verses, apportioned into six categories:

let us go on to perfection. There is a lesson here for us to learn— although they were spiritually infants, St. Paul did not lose hope in them but encouraged them to grow and move on to perfection. The first step is to leave behind the elementary teachings. This does not mean at all that the elementary teachings are not important. By no means is St. Paul saying that. They are the foundations of our beliefs. But they cannot remain stagnant at this basic spiritual level of understanding indefinitely. They have to build upon this foundation eventually.

laying again the foundation. The six foundational concepts laid out here are in a specific order. (1) Repentance from dead works. (2) Faith in God. (3) Baptism. (4) Laying on of hands. (5) Resurrection of the dead. (6) Eternal judgment.

of repentance from dead works and of faith toward God. (1 & 2) of 6. The first two steps when you preach to a non-believer is teaching them the need for repentance and to believe in Christ (who is the source of forgiveness for the sins which we repent).

of the doctrine of baptisms. (3) of 6. The next step for a person who intends on becoming Christian is to be baptized. ❖ The reason this word (*"baptisms"*) is plural is to reflect a concept that persisted during that time, trying to understand the difference between St. John the Baptist's baptism and the Baptism of the New Testament Christian Church. They were teaching that the baptism of John was a baptism of repentance only, but it was not the baptism of the new Church. *"And he said to them, 'Into what then were you baptized?' So they said, 'Into John's baptism.' Then Paul said, 'John indeed baptized with a baptism of repentance, saying to the people that they should believe on Him who would come after him, that is, on Christ Jesus.' When they heard this, they were baptized in the name of the Lord Jesus"* (Acts 19:3-5).

of laying on of hands. (4) of 6. After a person is baptized, they must receive the Holy Spirit, which during the Early Church was given solely by the *"laying on of hands."* Now, the Holy Spirit is usually relayed by the Myron oil (and actually, during Baptism, the person receives the Holy Spirit in three ways: the Myron Oil, the laying on of hands, and the breath of the Holy Spirit). Because oil is used, we often refer to this Mystery as "Chrismation" (the root word "Chrism" is derived from the Greek word *khrisma* which means "anointing.") The phrase *"laying on of hands"* refers to more than just Chrismation, however, but it also can be understood to signify the gift of the priesthood (bishops and priests) by which they are entitled to impart the Holy Spirit to effectuate the remaining Mysteries of the Church. Bishops and priests are ordained by the laying on of hands, and are then given the gift to invoke the Holy Spirit to administer the Mysteries. The rest of the Mysteries involve the Myron Oil if not also the laying on of hands, such as the Mystery of the Unction of the Sick.

of resurrection of the dead. (5) of 6. It is very important for the believer to believe in the resurrection of the dead. St. Paul said, *"Now if Christ is preached that He has been raised from the dead, how do some among you say that there is no resurrection of the dead? But if there is no resurrection of the dead, then Christ is not risen. And if Christ is not risen, then our preaching is empty and your faith is also empty"* (1 Cor. 15:12-14). And that is why we conclude the Orthodox creed in the following manner: *"We look for the resurrection of the dead, and the life of age to come."*

and of eternal judgment. (6) of 6. In the Orthodox Creed, we recite, *"He is coming again in His glory to judge the living and the dead."* Knowing we will stand before the judgment seat of God to give an account for our sins and deeds, we will be motivated to continue progressing in our struggle against Satan and against sin.

6:3 And this we will do. *"This"* refers to going on to perfection. At this point, St. Paul will proceed by speaking about spiritual matters beyond merely the elementary principles of Christianity.

if God permits. Spiritual progress towards perfection has to be according to the will of God and with the assistance of the grace of the Holy Spirit. What is perfection? It is not only growing, but it also involves remaining steadfast in your faith in Christ until the end, as He, Himself, said: *"He who endures to the end shall be saved"* (Matt. 24:13; Mark 13:13). Many people grow spiritually, but so many of them *"fall away,"* as St. Paul discusses later (Heb. 6:6). As already mentioned, the problem with the Hebrews is their apostasy, being tempted to return back to their former practices in Judaism. That is why St. Paul was encouraging them to continue steadfastly in Christ.

6:4-8 These are some of the most difficult verses to comprehend in the entire Bible. Many people interpret these verses in a variety of different ways. Some read it as saying, "It is impossible for those who have fallen away due to the sin of apostasy to return back to Christ and repent again." Let us see what the Church Fathers say about these verses. I want to differentiate between what is theologically impossible, and what is practically impossible. Theologically, there is no sin without forgiveness except the sin without repentance (i.e., for which a person has not repented for). Any person, even if he leaves Christianity to become a Jew or a worshipper of idols, can return back to Christianity and will be accepted by God, as the Lord promised: *"The one who comes to Me I will by no means cast out"* (John 6:37). Thus, theologically it is possible for apostates to repent and be accepted again. However, practically speaking, what does experience tell us about those who turn away from Christianity? When people return back to their formal religion, experience teaches us that it is practically impossible, especially for those who reached a very high degree of spiritual maturity as Christians before their apostasy (those who were once enlightened [through Baptism], who have tasted the heavenly gift [the Eucharist], who have become partakers of the Holy Spirit [Chrismation], who have tasted the goodness of the word of God, and who have tasted the powers of the age to come). When such people return back to their former religion or otherwise fall away from God, it is practically impossible for them to repent. Take the example of the heretic Arius. He was a priest in Alexandria and was a very eloquent preacher with a very extensive amount of knowledge. But when he fell into his heresy and denied the divinity of Christ, this was like apostasy and therefore it became practically impossible for him to repent, and he never did. Just for the sake of this example, let us assume he repented, he would have definitely been accepted and forgiven. Thus, these verses are not speaking about the possibility of returning to Christ theologically, but rather practically.

6:4 For it is impossible for those who were. As discussed regarding Hebrews 6:3, we must remain steadfast in our faith in Christ until the end. Why? Because for those who have become entrenched in the spiritual and intellectual richness of Christianity, it will be, practically speaking, impossible for them to return to Christianity once more.

✤ Note that St. Paul, in the following few verses, indirectly gave us a definition for those who are spiritually mature (having explained such people are practically not going to be able to return to Christianity if they fall away from it).

once enlightened. (1) The spiritually mature are enlightened, which refers to Baptism, which is also given the name the Mystery of Enlightenment, by which we move from darkness to light. But St. John Chrysostom said that not every baptized person is enlightened. Those who practice baptism as simply a rite or routine without living a life commensurate with one's baptism will not be considered enlightened. Baptism is to die with Christ and to live with Him. Maybe you were technically baptized, but if you are not dead to the world and living with Christ, then you will not experience the Mystery of Enlightenment.

have tasted the heavenly gift. (2) This refers to the Eucharist, the body and blood of Christ, who is the Bread that came down from heaven (as He said in John 6). There is a song sung sometimes during communion that calls the Eucharist the "Gift of gifts, and the Mystery of mysteries."

have become partakers of the Holy Spirit. (3) This refers to those who have received and been filled with the Holy Spirit by means of the Mystery of Chrismation, whereby a person becomes the temple of God. *"Or do you not know that your body is the temple of the Holy Spirit who is in you, whom you have from God, and you are not your own?"* (1 Corinthians 6:19).

6:5 have tasted the good word of God. This refers to those who study the Scriptures and keep it in their hearts, living by the word of God.

the powers of the age to come. This refers to those who witnessed such things as miracles, and also those who observed the transformational power of Christ's resurrection in the life of believers and in their own life. ✤ And here I want to mention that some denominations teach that a believer cannot perish once they have taken that initial step of faith in Christ; once you believe, you are saved. What about all these people that St. Paul is talking about who are not just simply believers, but are spiritually mature Christians. Yet, nonetheless, they can still *"fall away"* (Heb. 6:6).

6:6 if they fall away, to renew them again to repentance, since they crucify again for themselves the Son of God, and put Him to an open shame. When St. Paul said here, *"if they fall away,"* this does not refer to just any sin, but rather to apostasy, returning back to their former beliefs. Apostasy is not simply out of ignorance or mere error; instead, it refers to those who deliberately turn away from God. Here St. Paul is trying to tell them, if you consider returning back to Judaism after achieving spiritual maturity, you will have a nearly impossible time becoming Christian again. He compared such a situation to the Jews who heard the preaching of the Lord, saw His miracles, but in spite of this, they crucified Him. That is why he says, *"since they crucify again for themselves the Son of God, and put Him to an open shame."*

renew them again ... crucify again. The first time we were baptized, we participated in the crucifixion of our Lord Jesus Christ. If a person falls away, returning back to their former beliefs and rejecting their baptism, it is as if they are crucifying the Lord a second time. That is why St. John Chrysostom says that this verse refers to Baptism, because the Mystery of Baptism is a Mystery of renewal. So we can read this as saying, "If they fall again, it is impossible to re-baptize them again to repentance, since they crucify again (which is exactly what baptism—dying with Christ, being buried under the water, and then rising from it with His resurrection)." This is why Baptism is not to be repeated. If a person falls away, it is through repentance, not through Baptism, that a person may return to Christ. As St. Paul said in Ephesians Chapter 4, *"one faith, one baptism."* Hence, Baptism cannot be repeated so long as it is in the same faith. However, if a person is baptized in the wrong faith, such as the baptisms performed by heretics, it is no longer considered a proper baptism. If it is not based on sound faith, it is not part of that *"one faith"* and *"one baptism"* spoken of here.

✠ Note that in the Synaxarium on the 12th of Kiahk we commemorate the assembly of a council in Rome against the heresy of Novatus (also known as Benates) which was held in 249 A.D. Novatus utilized this specific verse to say that those who forsook the faith in the time of persecution will not be accepted again when they repent, as well as those who commit fornication; but the fathers replied and explained to him that the Apostle did not say this concerning the man who repents but concerning the man who intends to be baptized every time he is fallen into sin, for baptism can be carried on only once; as crucifixion only happened once so it is for baptism. As for the door to repentance, it is open to every repentant, otherwise everyone who falls in the sin of denying Christ or sins again will not be accepted even if he repents. They cited the example of St. Peter's repentance and how Christ came to the world to save sinners and lead them to repentance (Luke 13:3). Novatus refused to relinquish his opinion and thus the council exiled and excommunicated him and all that believe in his teachings.

✞ St. John Chrysostom ✞

Remarks on Heb. 6:9, 14

But what is "crucifying afresh"? [It is] crucifying over again. For as Christ died on the cross, so do we in baptism, not as to the flesh, but as to sin. Behold two deaths. He died as to the flesh; in our case the old man was buried, and the new man arose, made conformable to the likeness of His death. If therefore it is necessary to be baptized [again], it is necessary that this same [Christ] should die again. For baptism is nothing else than the putting to death of the baptized, and his rising again. And he well said, *"crucifying afresh unto themselves."* For he that does this, as having forgotten the former grace, and ordering his own life carelessly, acts in all respects as if there were another baptism. It behooves us therefore to take heed and to make ourselves safe. . . . On two grounds then he said that the thing was impossible, and he put the stronger last: first, because he who has been deemed worthy of such [blessings], and who has betrayed all that was granted to him, is not worthy to be again renewed; neither is it possible that [Christ] should again be crucified afresh: for this is to *"put Him to an open shame."* There is not then any second laver: there is not [indeed]. And if there is, there is also a third, and a fourth; for the former one is continually disannulled by the later, and this continually by another, and so on without end.

- Homily 9 on Hebrews, § 6-7

6:8 For the earth which drinks in the rain that often comes upon it, and bears herbs useful for those by whom it is cultivated, receives blessing from God; but if it bears thorns and briers, it is rejected and near to being cursed, whose end is to be burned. Here St. Paul elaborates further on why it is practically impossible for those who apostatize to return back to Christianity. St. Paul describes the believer like a plot of land, and the grace of God is analogized as being the rain that falls on this land. He is saying, this land that received the rain—the grace of God—was expected to bring forth useful plants (and we too, if we receive the grace of God and bear good fruit, we will receive additional blessings from Him). However, if after receiving the Holy Spirit (that is the grace of God—the rain), if I then bear *"thorns and briers,"* which can be regarded as sins, but especially in this verse is referring to apostasy, the land will be *"rejected and near to being cursed."*

near to being cursed. Here I want to emphasize the word *"near."* St. Paul said *"near,"* not simply that it is *"cursed."* The distinction here highlights the fact that St. Paul distinguishes between theoretical and practical impossibility for an apostate to return to his former Christian faith. Theologically, there is a possibility for repentance, but practically, it is impossible; that is why St. Paul said such a person is *"near"* to being cursed—practically, he is cursed, as he will most likely not return, but there is always a glimmer of hope that this person's heart will be moved to repent from their ways.

6:9-10 After this difficult message, the people needed a word of encouragement and support. So here, St. Paul as a clever physician, after rebuking them, he begins to give them words of motivation.

6:9 Beloved ... though we spoke in this manner. He uses this word to indicate to them that he was speaking about apostates, but they are not apostates to whom he is speaking. By the way, people will live up to (at the most, usually) the standard you expect of them. So if you have children and expect them to be bad children, they will be bad, or if you expect them to be good, they will be good. That is why St. Paul is setting the expectation of them that they will remain steadfast to the end, which is why he calls them *"beloved."* Although he "spoke in" the "manner" of rebuking them and telling them about their spiritual immaturity and infancy, yet in spite of all of this, St. Paul is confident in them.

we are confident of better things concerning you, yes, things that accompany salvation. We are confident that you will not apostatize.

But is the word "confident" here simply a compliment? St. Paul, as an apostle, is expected to be *"speaking the truth in love"* (Eph. 4:15), so we are not expecting St. Paul to be giving them an empty compliment lacking a genuine spirit behind it. No, but when St. Paul says he is confident, he really means what he says. Why, then, is that the case? This confidence is rooted in the notion that those who remain steadfast to the end will be saved.

6:10 For God is not unjust to forget your work and labor of love which you have shown toward His name. The confidence St. Paul has in their ability to remain steadfast in the faith and in the outcome of their beliefs—their salvation—is based on two things: the justice of God (*"For God is not unjust"*), and also their *"work and labor of love"* (which was directed toward God and also those in need).

the saints. The *"saints"* here refers to those in need, whom we like to refer to as the *"brethren of the Lord,"* as the Lord Christ said, *"Assuredly, I say to you, inasmuch as you did it to one of the least of these My brethren, you did it to Me"* (Matt. 25:40).

in that you have ministered ... and do minister. This refers to works of mercy such as the following: serving the poor and those in need, providing food for the hungry, visiting those in prison, giving drink to the thirsty, distributing clothes to the naked. This they did and continued to do. Such good works did not cease in their lives, nor was it simply a one-time occurrence. ✤ We should take from this a very important lesson. Recall in Matthew 25, when the Lord separated the righteous from the wicked, on what basis did He distinguish between them? Their good works, as we say in the Divine Liturgy and to which it is alluded in the Bible several times, *"He has appointed a Day for recompense, on which He will appear to judge the world in righteousness, and give each one according to his deeds."* And St. Paul is emphasizing here the importance of good deeds and good works in attaining salvation.

6:11-12 And we desire that each one of you show the same diligence to the full assurance of hope until the end, that you do not become sluggish, but imitate those who through faith and patience. St. Paul begins now to explain to them how they can persevere to the end and keep from being sluggish in their spiritual path. He describes two remedies to avoid becoming sluggish—an antidote of sorts: (1) Diligence until the end. (2) Imitate those who inherit the promises. This latter point refers to the saints who have perfected their lives in Christ; St. Paul is here setting the stage for Chapter 11, where he will speak of *"men of faith."* Such saints were described as having two qualities: faith and perseverance (*"patience"*). Thus, when we start to become lazy and *"lukewarm"* (Rev. 3:16), we should regain our composure by imitating the saints who through faith and patience endured to the end, and this will give me increased zeal and fervor in my heart, motivating me to continue with diligence to the end. That is why during almost every Divine Liturgy we hear the Synaxarion being read, which is a compilation of the stories of the saints. The readings from the Bible which we hear are the word of God that we should act upon. The Synaxarion is the living word of God—the word of God displayed in action, exhibiting how God's word was applied in the lives of the saints. When we remain diligent and imitate the saints, the end result (or fruit) will be the *"full assurance of hope."* When St. Paul tells the recipients of this epistle to show diligence *"to the full assurance of hope,"* the word *"to"* here can be read to say *"bear,"* so that St. Paul is asking the Jews to remain diligent in order to bear (or exhibit confidence in) the full assurance of hope.

inherit the promises. God promised us that we would receive an inheritance, which is eternal life. St. Paul is, thus, motivating them, saying that if you proceed in a manner of diligence and imitation of the saints, then you will inherit eternal life. Then he used the example of Abraham to support this notion in the next few verses.

6:13-20 St. Paul used the example of Abraham to indicate the reliability of the Lord's promises, and thus, by extension, a person's "full assurance" can be placed in any promises made by God. St. Paul will also use this example to return back to the subject of Christ having been promised as being the High Priest according to the order of Melchizedek, preparing the way for that discussion in Chapter 7.

6:13 **For when God made a promise to Abraham.** Which promise is St. Paul referring to? At least two: one promise was that God would give Abraham a son (Isaac) through his wife Sarah (Gen. 12:2-3); another promise involves the moment that Abraham was about to kill his son Isaac as an offering to God, at which time God stopped him and said, *"By Myself I have sworn, says the LORD, because you have done this thing, and have not withheld your son, your only son—blessing I will bless you, and multiplying I will multiply your descendants as the stars of the heaven and as the sand which is on the seashore; and your descendants shall possess the gate of their enemies"* (Gen. 22:16-17).

because He could swear by no one greater, He swore by Himself. God swore by the highest power available to Him, which is Himself. When God wanted to make an oath, He did not find a greater person than Himself to make this promise. God here is the one who swore the oath and also guaranteed it as well (because when you swear by someone or something, your oath is guaranteed by the same).

6:14 saying, "Surely blessing I will bless you, and multiplying I will multiply you." St. Paul is saying, then, "You Hebrews, the descendants of Isaac, the fact that you are living today is the strongest evidence of the fact that this promise of God was fulfilled."

6:15 And so, after he had patiently endured, he obtained the promise. St. Paul is giving them a hint: in order to obtain the promise, you need patience as well as endurance—perseverance. Thus, if God promises something, it will be fulfilled no matter what anyone thinks. If for some reason a person questions whether this is true, maybe they are lacking patience, or maybe we are not enduring adequately. Let us recall what St. Paul said in Hebrews Chapter 4, verse 1: *"Since a promise remains of entering His rest, let us fear lest any of you seem to have come short of it."* Hence, there is a promise here, and St. Paul is saying that God will keep it, but you must endure and be patient, or otherwise, we will fall short of such a promise.

6:16 For men indeed swear by the greater. Usually when a person makes an oath, they swear by something greater rather than lesser, but, as explained before, God could not find anyone greater than Himself and so, thus, *"swore by Himself."*

and an oath for confirmation is for them an end of all dispute. If there is a dispute between two men, then they refer back to the oath they made previously (or a new oath they make to resolve the dispute) will settle their differences.

6:17 Thus God, determining to show more abundantly to the heirs of promise the immutability of His counsel, confirmed it by an oath. St. Paul is saying, as men used the oath in order to end any dispute, then God, in order to affirm to us (the heirs of the promise) the reliability of His promises, He secured His promise with an oath by Himself.

more abundantly. God does not need to swear, because any word He says is true. But in order to show things more abundantly, because of our weakness as evinced by our lack of faith, God secured an oath for us.

immutability. This can be read as saying, roughly, as the "non-changeability." It refers to God as being one who is not changeable over time—He *"is* *the same yesterday, today, and forever"* (Heb. 13:8). We say in the Gregorian Liturgy that *"it is fitting indeed and right"* to praise God, and then go on to a list a number of characteristics: invisible, infinite, without beginning, everlasting, timeless, immeasurable, incomprehensible, and unchangeable, among other things.

6:18 **that by two immutable things, in which it is impossible for God to lie, we might have strong consolation.** What are the two unchangeable aspects of God that make His oath and promise secure? First, His word is itself unchangeable. If God says a word, it is unchangeable. Second, God's oath is unchangeable. God did not only use His words, but He also used an oath, so that by these *"two immutable things, in which it is impossible for God to lie, we might have strong consolation."* These two things, then, were given for us, because we are weak and may have doubts. Thus, He confirmed His promise to us.

who have fled for refuge to lay hold of the hope set before us. St. Paul is saying that in our life on earth, there are many challenges, hardships, and difficulties that may shake our faith. But when I know that God swore by Himself to give me the inheritance of eternal life, then I will find consolation. And in this promise, we can find refuge, to which I will flee to find safety and security. The practical import of St. Paul's message is as follows: when we have doubts, we should flee to the word of God and His promises, where we will *"lay hold of the hope set before us."* The city of our refuge is the word and promises of God. When you study the Bible, highlight all the promises of God so that whenever there is any doubt, agitation, or other sort of attack on your thoughts, return back to God's promises which were secured by His oath, and these promises will give you consolation, comfort, and rest.

6:19 **This hope we have as an anchor of the soul, both sure and steadfast.** The ship needs an anchor in order that it does not drift away, because without an anchor the ship will drift away and will suffer destruction. In a similar way, in the sea of this world, we are like the ship, but what is the anchor that we have to lay hold onto? The anchor is the hope we have in the promises of God, which are both trusted (*"sure"*) and unchangeable (*"steadfast"*).

and which enters the Presence behind the veil. In the tabernacle, there was a veil separating the middle of the three-section place of worship from the furthest section, the Holy of Holies. Thus, this verse is telling us that our hope in God and His promises opened the path to the very presence of God in the Holy of Holies, which is likened to the kingdom of heaven.).

6:20 **where the forerunner has entered for us, even Jesus, having become High Priest forever according to the order of Melchizedek.** What is the guarantee that, if we lay hope on God's promises, we will find salvation in heaven? The Lord Jesus Christ, the firstborn, the first fruit, entered as a *"forerunner"* to prepare the way for us, and because He became a brother among us and was not ashamed to call us His brethren, as He entered behind the veil, so also we will enter behind the veil too (which is heaven). St. Paul is speaking to Jews who know very well that the only person allowed to enter into the Holy of Holies, behind the veil, is the high priest. Thus, if Jesus entered behind the veil, then He is a high priest, but He is the High Priest after the order of Melchizedek rather than the order of Aaron. He entered "for us," referring to the role of the high priest in interceding on behalf of the people, which Christ Himself did. Since only the high priest could enter that inner sanctuary, and since the Lord Jesus is there on the right hand of God, Christ is the ultimate High Priest. ❖ Note that in this portion of St. Paul's epistle, St. Paul is subtly making reference to Psalm 110:4 where we find God the Father making a promise to Christ: The LORD has sworn and will not relent, *"You are a priest forever according to the order of Melchizedek."*

The past few verses and this one can be linked together as follows: As God was faithful in His promise to Abraham, He is also faithful in His promise to Christ that He would be a priest forever, after the order of Melchizedek. He is setting the stage here for Chapter 7 where he speaks about the high priesthood of Christ.

Chapter 6 Questions

1. What is apostasy? Why is it impossible from a practical standpoint to restore apostates to the Christian faith and practice?

2. If we take seriously the exhortation to exercise both faith and patience, what effect does that have on our Christian life?

3. In what sense have we "fled to a place of refuge"?

7

Chapter Outline

- Melchizedek the high priest (1-10)
- The eternal priesthood of Christ (11-25)
- The ultimate uniqueness of Christ (26-28)

Introduction

St. Paul concluded the previous chapter by making reference to Abraham and also setting the stage to speak about Christ's high priesthood being after the order of Melchizedek rather than the order of Aaron in this chapter. He starts this chapter by referring to Abraham's encounter with Melchizedek. Before delving right away into that story, it is important to realize that St. Paul started to speak about Christ as being a priest beginning with Chapter 2 of this epistle. Hebrews 2:17 was the first time that St. Paul referred to Christ as a priest. Hebrews 4:14 focuses on Christ as our High Priest. In Hebrews 5:16, St. Paul quotes Psalm 110:4, in which the Psalmist describes Christ's priesthood being after the order of Melchizedek. In Chapter 7, St. Paul will elaborate as to what it means to be a priest according to the order of Melchizedek, distinguishing it from Levitical priesthood.

7:1 For this Melchizedek ... who met Abraham returning from the slaughter of the kings. He is referring to a story mentioned in Genesis Chapter 14 when Abraham heard that four kings occupied Sodom and Gomorrah and took Lot (the nephew of Abraham) as a captive there. So Abraham took his servants, fought against these kings, and through the power of God, he was able to defeat them. Then, when he returned from the slaughter of these kings, Melchizedek met him.

priest of the Most High God. The first observation to which I would like to draw your attention with respect to Melchizedek is that he was a king while at the same time a priest as well. Usually, if you study the nation of Israel, the kings were from the tribe of Judah, and the priests were descendants of Levi. Thus, it was virtually impossible to find in the history of Israel a person who was both a king and a priest. Melchizedek was both a king and a priest, which is akin to Christ who is the King of kings and the Priest of priests.

king of Salem. Virtually all the ancient scholars and Church Fathers said that Salem referred to Jerusalem; however, some modern scholars say that Salem is the city of Shechem (a city whose name is mentioned throughout the Scriptures). Regardless, Melchizedek was the king of the city called *"Salem,"* and met Abraham.

and blessed him. Here begins a

discussion of the various aspects of Melchizedek that evinces his role as a priest. First, you find him blessing Abraham. If Melchizedek blessed Abraham, then who is superior? Melchizedek or Abraham? Obviously, it is Melchizedek, because normally the lesser is the one who is blessed by one who is superior.

7:2 to whom also Abraham gave a tenth part of all. Usually priests collect the tithes of the people, which was a role assigned later—specifically to the Levites. Abraham gave his tithes to Melchizedek, which indicates that Melchizedek is to be regarded as a priest for Abraham. Moreover, recall that in the story of the meeting between Abraham and Melchizedek, this king and priest offered to Abraham *"bread and wine"* (Gen. 14:8). I am sure when you read that, your mind immediately connects it with the Mystical Supper. Hence, we have three aspects that exhibit Melchizedek's priestly role as well as his superiority to Abraham: blessing Abraham, offering bread and wine, and receiving tithes.

first being translated "king of righteousness," and then also king of Salem, meaning "king of peace." St. Paul explains the meaning of the name Melchizedek, which literally is translated king (from "Melchi") of righteousness (from "zedek"). This king can also be called the *"king of peace,"* as the city of which he is said to be king, Salem, is very close to the word "Shalom" in Hebrew which means peace. By his name and position, we can then deduce that this Melchizedek is both a king of righteousness and of peace. And this is again akin to the Lord Jesus Christ who is rightly called the King of Righteousness and of peace as well.

7:3 without father, without mother, without genealogy. This can be a very difficult verse to understand. Some people like to interpret this verse as if saying that Melchizedek is one of the appearances of the hypostasis of the Son in the Old Testament, as if Christ appeared in the form of this king. Some other scholars of the Bible like to try to draw a connection between Melchizedek and the Archangel Michael. But the interpretation according to the Church Fathers is that he was a regular human being, not an appearance of the Son of God or the Archangel Michael. This verse is then to be understood in a typological (symbolic) way. As you know in the Old Testament, genealogy was very important. For example, the first nine chapters of 1 Chronicles is all about genealogy. They want to maintain such records, especially if they are priests, in order to trace their lineage to Levi, whose descendants were the only ones permitted to be priests. So, for priests, this is particularly important. And also they wanted to know from which tribe the Messiah would come. But when the story of Melchizedek was mentioned in the book of Genesis, there was no genealogy accompanying his story, and so his mention in the Scriptures seemed to come out of nowhere, with no details given to describe his past or his future. That is why St. Paul says here that we do not know who his father is and who is mother is (not that he was not born of a human father and mother).

having neither beginning of days nor end of life. In speaking about the right of priesthood according to the order of Melchizedek, there is no mention in the Bible about when his priesthood started or when it ended. If you compare this with the Levitical priesthood, we know when it started (by Aaron) and also when it ended (when the temple was destroyed). Even to this day, it is very difficult for the Jews to determine who are the descendants of Aaron. That is why there is a big problem for them now, because according to Jewish Scripture and rites, priests can only be selected from among the Levites. But when we speak about the priesthood of Melchizedek, we cannot find his beginning nor his end spoken of in the Bible. (Recall that, with regard to having no end to his priesthood, what the Psalmist says in Psalm 110:4— that the priesthood of Melchizedek is regarded as having no end: *"You are a priest forever according to the order of Melchizedek."*)

but made like the Son of God, remains a priest continually. Here we have to ask ourselves a question. The Bible, which emphasizes the importance of maintaining genealogy, why was Melchizedek's genealogy left out? *"But made like the Son of God."* The Holy Spirit, who inspired Moses in writing the Book of Genesis, prohibited Moses from mentioning anything about the genealogy of Melchizedek in order to allow for him to be a type (or symbol) of Jesus Christ. Christ, who came as a priest after the order of Melchizedek, also, as Son of God, did not have a father or mother from the tribe of Levi to establish His claim to priesthood, and thus, His priesthood has no beginning and also remains continually. Later, St. Paul will explain why the eternal feature of Christ's priesthood is so important, as distinguished from the transient nature of the Levitical priesthood.

7:4 Now consider how great this man was, to whom even the patriarch Abraham gave a tenth of the spoils. After St. Paul introduced for us the person of Melchizedek, now he wants us to reflect upon his greatness and uniqueness. The argument now that St. Paul will make is to prove to us the superiority of Melchizedek. If St. Paul can prove that the priesthood of Melchizedek is superior to that of the Levites, then the priesthood of Christ, which is after the order of Melchizedek, is also superior. The main theme of the letter to the Hebrews was to warn them against apostasy, fearing the Jewish Christians would return back to Judaism. That is why St. Paul wanted to tell them, no, as a Christian, your Lord Jesus Christ is a priest that is superior to the Levites. St. Paul begins this argument by recalling the fact that Melchizedek was so great that even the famed patriarch (meaning the "head father" or "father of fathers") of Israel, Abraham, gave a tenth of his spoils to him. If Abraham is the patriarch of Israel, being the head father of Israel, then Melchizedek, being superior to Abraham, is the head of the father of fathers.

7:5 And indeed those who are of the sons of Levi, who receive the priesthood, have a commandment to receive tithes from the people according to the law, that is, from their brethren, though they have come from the loins of Abraham. Not all the sons of Levi were priests. That appointment was reserved for only the sons of Aaron. So the other sons of Levi served in other ways. According to the Old Testament, they were tasked with receiving tithes from the people, even from their own brethren. St. Paul says here that, since they are brethren, they are in a sense equal, all being descendants from Abraham; however, because they are given a special rank among their brethren, they are no longer to be regarded as equals, but in a sense superior to their brethren.

7:6 but he whose genealogy is not derived from them received tithes from Abraham . Melchizedek is not related to Abraham at all, obviously. Those who were brethren (the Levites being related to the rest of the Israelites due to the fact that all of them were descendants of Abraham), when some of them became priests, they became superior to their brethren (the other tribes of Israel). Now consider how great Melchizedek was who, not being related to Abraham, and therefore not even considered to be among their brethren, yet he took tithes from their ancestor Abraham.

and blessed him. Not only did he receive tithes from Abraham, but he blessed him too. (See verse 9 for more on this.)

who had the promises. In the previous chapter, Abraham was regarded as the man of promises. This great man that God swore promises to—Abraham—was blessed by Melchizedek. Hence, again, it is being emphasized the extent to which Melchizedek is greater than Abraham.

7:7 Now beyond all contradiction the lesser is blessed by the better. St. Paul is trying to appeal to common

7:8 Here mortal men receive tithes, but there [H]e receives them, of whom it is witnessed that [H]e lives. This verse can yet again be deemed confusing. St. Paul is saying *"here,"* in the Levitical priesthood system, mortal men receive tithes (because all the priests of the tribe of Levi are mortal), but *"there"* (referring to the priesthood after the order of Melchizedek), He (referring to Christ) receives tithes, of whom it is witnessed that He (Christ) lives forever. St. Paul, in this chapter, will reference the resurrection of Christ to exhibit how Christ the High Priest is immortal and thus, lives forever. This is another reason we should consider that the priesthood of Melchizedek (which is continued in the person of Christ who lives forever) is greater than the priesthood of the Levites (whose priests are mortal).

7:9-10 Even Levi, who receives tithes, paid tithes through Abraham, so to speak, for he was still in the loins of his father when Melchizedek met him. Think about this: before Levi and Aaron were born, they were in a sense still in *"the loins of*

sense and rational thinking, that the superior blesses the inferior, and that Melchizedek is thus superior to Abraham.

Abraham." When Melchizedek blessed Abraham, he also blessed those who were still in his loins: Levi and Aaron. Also, one can consider that when Abraham paid tithes to Melchizedek, that Levi and Aaron also in a sense paid tithes to Melchizedek too. Therefore, one can consider Melchizedek the priest of priests, and by extension, the priesthood of Christ as being superior to that of the Levites.

7:11-12 Therefore, if perfection were through the Levitical priesthood (for under it the people received the law), what further need was there that another priest should rise according to the order of Melchizedek, and not be called according to the order of Aaron? For the priesthood being changed, of necessity there is also a change of the law. St. Paul begins now to discuss the reason God put in place two systems of priesthood—the Levitical priesthood, and that according to the order of Melchizedek. When St. Paul says the word *"perfection,"* that word can be translated to mean fulfillment of a goal, or accomplishment of a task. Thus, we can read this verse as saying, "If God's goal for all of us to be saved was accomplished according to the order of the Levitical priesthood, then why would another order of priesthood be needed?" Levitical priesthood failed to fulfill and accomplish the goal of God in saving the human race.

For that reason, there was a need for another system of priesthood to be implemented. Since the old system of priesthood was instituted according to the law of the Old Testament, then the new system of priesthood requires a new law to be set in place of the old.

Law. St. Paul, in this verse, is not referring to the entire Old Testament as needing to be revamped. He is referring to the regulations related to the Levitical priesthood.

7:13 **For He of whom these things are spoken belongs to another tribe, from which no man has officiated at the altar.** This refers to Christ who belonged to the tribe of Judah, and no man from this tribe has ever been given the rank of priesthood (*"no man has officiated at the altar"*). In the previous set of priestly regulations in the Old Testament, only a person of the tribe of Levi can be a priest. However, Christ, who is not a Levite by descent, but rather being of the tribe of Judah, is a priest according to another set of priestly regulations that has displaced the old. St. Paul responds to those who criticize his remarks that Christ is our High Priest by saying that His priesthood is according to a new set of rules and is superior to that which was previously set in place. Additionally, St. Paul here marks a distinction between Christ and other priests in that He is a priest while at the same time of the tribe from which kings descended—the tribe of Judah.

7:14 **For it is evident that our Lord arose from Judah, of which tribe Moses spoke nothing concerning priesthood.** Moses wrote nothing in his writings regarding the regulations of priesthood that a person can be a priest who is from the tribe of Judah.

7:15-17 **And it is yet far more evident if, in the likeness of Melchizedek, there arises another priest who has come, not according to the law of a fleshly commandment, but according to the power of an endless life. For He testifies: "You are a priest forever according to the order of Melchizedek."** St. Paul compares here between the priesthood of the Levites and that of Melchizedek by saying that the former is according to the laws of a fleshly commandment, while the latter is according to the *"power of an endless life."* Notice the contrast between the following words: law and power; fleshly and endless; commandment and life. When St. Paul said, *"law of a fleshly commandment,"* he is contrasting *"power,"* with *"law,"* *"endless,"* with *"fleshly,"* and *"life,"* with *"commandment."* Levitical priesthood came according to a set of regulations which gave commandments (or orders) for people to follow, which

St. Paul calls *"fleshly,"* which refers to the mortal and transient nature of Levitical priesthood. The priesthood of Christ, however, came about by power. To explain this, let me use the following analogy. With any kingdom on earth, the transfer of power usually occurs according to the laws or regulations understood in that kingdom, such as when a prince takes over the kingdom after his father's death. When there is a revolution, however, the person who takes over the kingdom after overthrowing its king becomes its leader not by law, but rather by power and might, since he fought for and won his position. Christ did not become a priest according to the law, but rather became so due to the power of His resurrection and His victory over Satan, and that is why He entered by His own blood into the Holy of Holies (which is heaven). His priesthood came by the power of His Cross and resurrection. This power was not temporary (as opposed to being fleshly—i.e., mortal), but exists eternally, as Christ trampled death by His death. Death could not hold Him. That is why His power gave Him endlessness. Hence, Christ's priesthood continues forever because it did not come about by any set of regulations but instead by His own power. The law gives commandments, but Christ's power gives life. Fleshly commandments can be overturned by newer ones, but Christ's power of an endless life will never be vanquished. The eternal character of Christ's priesthood was, thus, rightly attested to by the psalmist in Psalm 110:4: *"You are a priest forever according to the order of Melchizedek."*

7:18-19 For on the one hand there is an annulling of the former commandment because of its weakness and unprofitableness, for the law made nothing perfect; on the other hand, there is the bringing in of a better hope, through which we draw near to God. St. Paul has thus far made three arguments in the previous set of verses for the need and benefit of having a new priesthood: The Levitical form of the priesthood failed, and so because there is a need for another priesthood, there is a need for another law. Christ came from a different tribe, so His priesthood is definitely not after the order of Levi, but rather after some other order: that of Melchizedek. The priesthood of Christ is according to the power of an endless life, whereas the priesthood of the Levites is according to the law of a fleshly commandment. The next argument St. Paul makes is in this verse, saying that the former laws of the Levitical priesthood were weak and unprofitable in that they failed to fulfill (*"made nothing perfect"*) the goal of God in saving the human race and drawing us near to Him, but on the other hand, the priesthood of Christ is a *"bringing in of a better hope"* (see Chapter 6) through the power of the resurrection of Christ which gives us eternal life. Remember that the role of a priest is to bring the people closer to God as their intercessor, but the Levitical priesthood failed in this regard, because after all the holy men of Israel died, they went to Hades. However, the priesthood of Christ, because of His victory over death, Satan, and Hades, and because He entered us by His own blood into the Holy of the Holies (heaven) and took us all with Him there, was therefore able to fulfill God's goal in drawing us all near to God.

7:20-21 And inasmuch as He was not made priest without an oath ... but He with an oath by Him who said to Him: "The LORD has sworn and will not relent, 'You are a priest forever according to the order of Melchizedek.'" He is again referring to Psalm 110:4, which he quotes in its entirety in v. 21. As explained in Chapter 6, God made a promise, and then swore to that oath by Himself, then both what He spoke and what He swore is unchangeable and reliable, since God is unchangeable and therefore, reliable. This promise, then, is permanent.

for they have become priests without an oath. Levitical priests became priests without making any oath, as simply being born from among the Levites and being a descendant of Aaron qualified them for the authority of priesthood.

7:22 by so much more Jesus has become a surety of a better covenant. Having laid out many arguments, St. Paul is now going to draw certain conclusions. If we believe in Christ and accepted His blood and through His intercession for us that He made by offering Himself as a sacrifice on the cross, holding to this hope we can put complete confidence in Christ that we will go to heaven with Him, in Him, and through Him. He swore by Himself and therefore, became a *"surety of a better covenant"* in that there is no one greater than God on whom we can rely as guaranteeing His own promise. He guaranteed that He is a priest forever, and swore an oath to Himself to this effect, as explained in the previous few verses; therefore, we have a true assuredness in Christ's salvation if we rely on Him.

covenant. Covenants, as explained more in Chapters 8 and 9, were made between people with a blood as its surety; but the new covenant was made by Christ's own blood: *"For this is My blood of the new covenant, which is shed for many for the remission of sins"* (Matt. 26:28).

7:23-24 Also there were many priests, because they were prevented by death from continuing. But He, because He continues forever, has an unchangeable priesthood. In the Old Testament, there was not only one priest, but many priests, because they were all mortal and thus, whenever they died, other priests had to take their place and continue that ministry. However, Christ, because He is immortal, His priesthood remains in Him and will never change to anyone else—He will remain a priest forever as death is no longer a hindrance that must be addressed as it had been previously. Now, because His priesthood is unchangeable, we have a better *"surety"* (Heb. 7:22), not only because of the superiority of His priesthood, but because His priesthood is unchangeable.

7:25 Therefore He is also able to save to the uttermost those who come to God through Him, since He always lives to make intercession for them. In this verse, St. Paul draws another conclusion. Not only is Christ *"a surety of a better covenant,"* but also through the priesthood of Christ, He is able to *"save to the uttermost those who come to God through Him."* He is the way of salvation: *"I am the way, the truth, and the life. No one comes to the Father except through Me"* (John 14:6). Christ is the only way to eternal life: *"Nor is there salvation in any other, for there is no other name under heaven given among men by which we must be saved"* (Acts 4:12). Christ always lives and therefore, can always serve as a priest, making intercession on behalf of all people who accept His priesthood. The priesthood of Christ is continuous, sitting at the right hand of the Father, interceding for us unceasingly by His blood to the Father. That is why He is *"able to save to the uttermost those who come to God through Him, since He always lives to make intercession for them."* Recalling the main theme of this epistle, where St. Paul was trying to persuade Jewish Christians not to succumb to the pressure to return back to Judaism, He is trying to tell them that if they return to Judaism, they are returning to a weaker system which failed in its attempt to accomplish God's place to save you; will you then still leave Christ, knowing that He is *"a surety of a better covenant"* (Heb. 7:22)? Will you still leave Christ, who is the only one *"able to save to the uttermost those who come to God through Him,"* since He lives forever? So, reconsider your decision, you who are considering to leave Christ.

7:26 For such a High Priest was fitting for us, who is holy, harmless, undefiled, separate from sinners, and has become higher than the heavens. St. Paul here begins to introduce a new idea: the priesthood of Melchizedek is superior to the priesthood of the Levites not only because of all the reasons mentioned above, but there is another reason: the person of the Lord Jesus Christ. Who Christ is—the Lord Christ and His characteristics—contributed to superiority of the priesthood according to the order of Melchizedek. Thus, St. Paul gives three descriptions as to the uniqueness of Christ as the ultimate High Priest:

holy. From a spiritual point of view, the Lord Jesus is holy, which means that He was all God wanted Him to be; He was loyal and obedient to the Father; He lived with integrity. He was unique in His being holy.

harmless. If holy describes the spiritual dimension of Christ, harmless describes the moral point of view about Christ, in that He is without evil.

undefiled. From a religious point of view, He is undefiled, which means nothing impure has attached itself to Him.

separate from sinners. He is separated from sinners because of His sinless perfection, and also because, by His ascension, He has become higher than the heavens, separating us from our horizon here which is full of sins and sinners.

7:27 who does not need daily, as those high priests, to offer up sacrifices, first for His own sins and then for the people's. Levitical priests needed to offer sacrifices every day: first, for their own sins, and then also for the sins of the people. But Christ, who is *"holy, harmless, undefiled, separate from sinners, and [who] has become higher than the heavens,"* does not need to offer any sacrifice for Himself.

for this He did once for all when He offered up Himself. Christ did not offer daily sacrifices, but rather offered one sacrifice for all time for all to partake of Him, those who are willing. And let me point out that the sacrifice on the altar which we present—the Eucharist—is not a new offering; rather, it is the same offering of Himself: *"This is the life-giving Flesh that Your only-begotten Son, our Lord, God, and Savior Jesus Christ, took from our Lady, the Lady of us all, the holy Theotokos, Saint Mary. . . . He gave It up for us upon the holy wood of the cross, of His own will, for us all."* We recall the sacrifice, relive it, and re-enter into it, every time we partake of the Eucharist. Who dares offer Christ? No one dares: Christ offered Himself. We declare this in the Liturgy: *"He loved His own who are in the world, and gave Himself up for our salvation unto death."*

once. Christ offered Himself only once because of His uniqueness in being holy, harmless, and undefiled, and also because His sacrifice of Himself was perfect—there is no better sacrifice than Himself, which then does not need repeating due to its completeness and the fact that there is nothing better to offer again. The need for repetition then has disappeared.

for all. This word, *"all,"* can refer to two things. Christ offered Himself once for all people, and it can also refer to the notion that Christ offered Himself once for all time.

7:28 For the law appoints as high priests men who have weakness, but the word of the oath, which came after the law, appoints the Son who has been perfected forever. St. Paul concludes his comparison of Christ and the Levitical priests by sharing four differences: (1) Levitical priests were appointed according to law, while Christ was appointed by an oath. (2) Levitical priests were chosen among men, while Christ is the Son of God who became Man. (3) Levitical priests exhibited weakness, but Christ has been perfected (in the sense that He accomplished the will of the Father). (4) Levitical priests were temporary, whose role was taken over by those who followed them after their death; Christ, however, is forever.

CHRIST	LEVITICAL PRIESTS
Appointed by an oath	Appointed by the law
Son of God who became man	Man
Has been perfected (accomplished the will of the Father)	Have weaknesses
Forever	Temporary

which came after the law. The oath that was mentioned in the Book of Psalms was expressed chronologically in the Scriptures after the books of the law were written by Moses. However, the oath itself from the Father to Christ was sworn to before all ages—an eternal oath.

Chapter 7 Questions

1. Why is the Lord Jesus the surety of a better covenant?

2. Why is the Lord Jesus able to save people "to the uttermost"?

3. What is the essential function of a priest?

4. How is the Lord Jesus described in verse 26?

5. How does the Lord Jesus differ from human high priests?

8

Chapter Outline

• Heavenly sanctuary (1-5)
• Better covenant (6-13)

Introduction

In the last chapter, St. Paul provided proof for the uniqueness of Christ as the superior High Priest, comparing Christ's priesthood after the order of Melchizedek with the Levitical priesthood of Israel. Christ, then, was proved to be greater than Aaron and any priest descending from him. Beginning in this chapter through Hebrews 10:18, St. Paul will continue to discuss the conclusion based on his previous arguments, that Christ is the High Priest of high priests, superior to and better than any other, presiding in a heavenly sanctuary rather than the inferior one in which Levitical priests used to serve in.

8:1 Now this is the main point of the things we are saying. He started by saying that *"this is the main point of the things we are saying."* Now we will come to the main point that I want to make—my conclusions drawn from my previous arguments.

We have such a High Priest, who is seated at the right hand of the throne of the Majesty in the heavens. If you remember in Hebrews 1:3, St. Paul spoke about Christ as sitting at the right hand of the Father, as the Son. But now He is saying that He is not only seated at the right hand of the Father as His son, but is sitting as the High Priest. St. Paul previously referred explicitly to Psalm 110:4 numerous times in this epistle. Here, St. Paul is implicitly referring to Psalm 110:1, which says: The LORD said to my Lord, *"Sit at My right hand, till I make Your enemies Your footstool."* The first mention of *"Lord"* here is God the Father, and the second mention of *"Lord"* refers to the Son. Hence, we can read this psalm as saying, "The Father said to His Son, *'Sit at my right hand.'"* Later, in verse 4, we read that the Father said to Christ that He is a priest forever according to the order of Melchizedek. So the Son now is seated at the right hand of the Father, not only as the Son but also as the High Priest.

8:2 a Minister. This letter was written in Greek. The original word which was translated to the English word *"Minister,"* was leitourgos (λειτουργὸς). This word should seem familiar to you, as the word *"liturgy"* is derived from this word. When we refer to the Divine Liturgy, we are usually focused on the Eucharist, which is presented by the priest. This word, then, does not refer to Christ's status as a minister or servant per se, but rather refers to His activity as the High Priest—He is a priest. Recall that the word Liturgy is derived from two Greek words which together literally mean "the work of the people" (*laos*—people; *ergon* or *ergos*—work), referring to public worship. Christ, then, being described as the "leitourgos" here makes reference to His role in leading us as our High Priest, interceding before the throne of God on behalf of His people. Christ's status is thus, in no way being described here; Christ is not a servant, but is the Son of God.

of the sanctuary and of the true tabernacle. Here, St. Paul compares between the earthly sanctuary (which is the Tabernacle of Meeting) and the heavenly sanctuary (described as the *"true tabernacle"*). The word sanctuary was used in the Old Testament to refer to the Holy of Holies. Notice that the word sanctuary comes fom the word sanctified, which is something set apart and declared as being holy. The Lord, as the High Priest, is in the Holy of the Holies, entering not into the earthly Holy of Holies, but rather the heavenly Holy of Holies, which is the true sanctuary, the true tabernacle.

true tabernacle ... which the Lord erected, and not man. Why is this heavenly sanctuary considered the *"true"* tabernacle? There are at least three reasons. The first is that it is heavenly, rather than earthly. The earthly tabernacle will pass away, and obviously the Temple of Solomon was destroyed a long time ago. The earthly tabernacle is temporary, but the heavenly tabernacle is eternal. The second reason why the heavenly sanctuary is considered the true tabernacle is that it was not made by man, but rather by God Himself. Finally, as mentioned in v. 5 below, the earthly tabernacle is simply a *"copy and shadow of the heavenly things."* When God asked Moses to build the tabernacle, after explaining in details its design, He showed Him in a vision what the heavenly tabernacle looks like. It was like a revelation, such as the one St. John experienced. The earthly tabernacle, then, was a copy and shadow of the heavenly one. When you read in the Book of Revelation you will find a description of the tabernacle: *"Then the temple of God was opened in heaven, and the ark of His covenant was seen in His temple. And there were lightnings, noises, thunderings, an earthquake, and great hail"* (Rev. 11:19). By making the heavenly tabernacle superior to the earthly one, St. Paul provides another reason why Christ's priesthood is superior to that of the Levites since He serves a superior place.

8:3 **For every high priest is appointed to offer both gifts and sacrifices.** The main role of the priesthood is to intercede on behalf of the people. How does the priest intercede? By offering gifts and sacrifices to God. Previously in this commentary, a differentiation was made between the term *"gifts"* and the term *"sacrifices."* Gifts do not involve the shedding of blood, while sacrifices do. In the Book of Leviticus, we read about the burnt offering, peace offering, sin offering, and trespass offering, all of which involve the shedding of blood and are thus, rightly regarded as sacrifices. As for other offerings, such as the grain offering (Lev. 2), they would be regarded as a gifts.

Therefore it is necessary that this One also have something to offer. If we are calling Christ a priest, then it makes sense to think about what it is He offers. Of course, we know that He offered Himself. That is why St. Cyril is known to have said that Christ is the High Priest and is also the Sacrifice which the High Priest offers, as we say in the hymn Fai Etaf-enf (Ⲫⲁⲓ ⲉⲧⲁϥⲉⲛϥ)—which begins as follows: *"This is He who presented Himself on the cross [as] an acceptable sacrifice."*

8:4 For if He were on earth, He would not be a priest, since there are priests who offer the gifts according to the law. If Christ attempted to be a priest while on earth, He would not be able to according to the Mosaic regulations set for the priesthood, because He was not a descendant of Aaron as the law requires. Christ is a descendant of the tribe of Judah. Hence, the fact that the Father said to the Son, "You are a priest" (Ps. 110:4), this means that since He is not technically qualified to be an earthly priest, then He must be a priest elsewhere: if not earth, then His priesthood must be heavenly.

8:5 who. Referring to the descendants of Aaron.

serve the copy and shadow of the heavenly things. Christ serves the true, genuine, authentic, heavenly tabernacle, whereas Levitical priests served a copy and shadow of that true tabernacle.

as Moses was divinely instructed when he was about to make the tabernacle. For He said, "See that you make all things according to the pattern shown you on the mountain." Moses saw a vision of the true tabernacle, which served as a basis for the design of the earthly one, thus making the earthly one merely a "copy" and "shadow" of the heavenly one.

8:6 ministry. See commentary on Heb. 8:2 above for more on this word.

But now He has obtained a more excellent ministry. His ministry is better than the ministry of the Levitical priesthood in the Old Testament.

inasmuch as He is also Mediator. St. Paul delves deeply into the priesthood of Christ. The relationship between God and us is a covenant relationship. There was a certain ritual practiced when a covenant was entered into (which you can read about in Genesis Chapter 15, when God made a covenant with Abraham). The parties entering into a covenant (as opposed to simply a contract, which is just an exchange of promises) used to take an animal, cut it in half, and then lay each half of the animal on either side of a path of blood (from the animal). This path was known as the "blood path," which both parties entering into a covenant would walk along together. This ritual signified that, unlike a contract, the penalty of breaking the covenant is death—the shedding of blood. With Abraham, there was a unique variation to the norm: only God, by Himself, walked down the blood path; He did not ask Abraham to walk with Him. This is because God, although He would definitely not break His own covenant, yet if Abraham were to falter, then Abraham would have had to die as punishment. Thus, when the children of Abraham broke the covenant with God, it was God who died on everyone's behalf in order to give us life. Hence, our relationship with God is a covenant relationship. When we break the covenant, who mediates between the sinner—the person that broke the covenant—and God? It is the priest. That is why in the Old Testament, whenever a person would commit a sin, they would take an animal and ask the priest to sacrifice it on the person's behalf. Levitical priests used to perform this mediation, but Christ, since He is serving in the true, genuine, heavenly, authentic sanctuary, His mediation is more excellent than the mediation of Levitical priests.

of a better covenant, which was established on better promises. St. Paul compares between the old covenant and the new covenant, *"which was established on better promises."* St. Paul will elaborate about this in more detail in the next set of verses (see three of the *"better promises"* which make the new covenant better, detailed in verses 10, 11, and 12). Before proceeding, let me explain the manner in which God established His covenant throughout the Old Testament. If we study how the first covenant was established, it was made between God and Adam, based on just a promise: *"And I will put enmity between you and the woman, and between your seed and her Seed; He shall bruise your head, and you shall bruise His heel"* (Gen. 3:15). Then, later, God renewed the covenant with Noah, at which time God did not only make a promise but also accompanied His promise with a sign in nature: *"I set My rainbow in the cloud, and it shall be for the sign of the covenant between Me and the earth. . . . The rainbow shall be in the cloud, and I will look on it to remember the everlasting covenant between God and every living creature of all flesh that is on the earth"* (Gen. 9:13,

16). God renewed the covenant yet again with Abraham with not simply a promise accompanied by a sign, but more than that: a promise with a sign in the flesh—which was circumcision (*"This is My covenant which you shall keep, between Me and you and your descendants after you: Every male child among you shall be circumcised; and you shall be circumcised in the flesh of your foreskins, and it shall be a sign of the covenant between Me and you."*—Gen. 17:10-11). Then with Moses, God renewed His covenant and gave another sign, which was the blood of animals: *"And Moses took the blood, sprinkled it on the people, and said, "This is the blood of the covenant which the LORD has made with you according to all these words"* (Ex. 24:8). In summary, the covenant was established by a promise, then by a sign in nature (rainbow), then a sign in the flesh (circumcision), and then the blood of animals. The new covenant is now established by the previous blood of the Son of God.

8:7 For if that first covenant had been faultless, then no place would have been sought for a second. The first covenant—the old covenant—was based on the righteousness of the law. You needed to keep the entire law, not to break any of its commandments. If you follow the entire law without violating any of its precepts, then you are righteous and can then enter into the covenant with God. The starting point for people then—their status—was that of a sinner. To progress toward righteousness, the entire law needed to be fulfilled. Unfortunately, no one was able to keep all the commandments of the law. That is why law—the old covenant—failed in the sense that people were not able to achieve righteousness by it. The new covenant, however, when we accept the Lord Christ and decide to turn our lives to Him, we are baptized and become a new nature in the Lord Christ. Our starting point is not the status of a sinner as in the Old Testament, but rather one who is righteous in Christ, as Ananias said to St. Paul: *"And now why are you waiting? Arise and be baptized, and wash away your sins, calling on the name of the Lord"* (Acts 22:16). This is why the newly baptized dons white clothes, to say that now you have put on the righteousness of Christ. This is a big difference: the old law said you have to do a certain set of things in order to become righteous, whereas in the New Testament, we begin with righteousness which we strive to maintain by refraining from sin and increasing in virtue. If you sin again, you go to Christ and wash your sins in the blood of the Lamb on the altar and then you are made righteous again. Hence, if the first covenant was *"faultless,"* able to sanctify us and give us righteousness, then there would have been no need for a second covenant to displace the first. But the fact that God spoke of a second covenant (in Jeremiah

31:31-34, which St. Paul quotes from in the ensuing verses), means the old covenant was faulty.

8:8-9 Because finding fault with them ... I disregarded them. Is the law in and of itself bad or faulty? No, as St. Paul said in his Epistle to the Romans: *"I agree with the law that it is good"* (Rom. 7:16). Rather, it is because of us, the sinners, who could not keep the commandments of God without breaking them. When God found us with fault, God spoke of a new covenant that would displace the old one. He did not create us to perish, but out of His great love He sought our salvation so that we may enjoy eternal life with Him. That is why there was a need for a *"a better covenant, which was established on better promises"* (Heb. 8:6).

He says. The verses that follow come from God's pronouncement through the prophet Jeremiah 31:31-34.

Behold, the days are coming, says the LORD. The *"days"* that *"are coming"* refers to the days of Christ—the incarnation of the Son of God.

when I will make a new covenant with the house of Israel and with the house of Judah. This refers to God's people in general, metaphorically speaking. It refers to all people who are willing to accept Christ and the conditions of this new covenant of which He speaks. Hence, this new covenant is not restricted merely to the house of Israel and the house of Judah, but was offered for all who desire to accept Christ (a point which will be elaborated more upon in Chapter 9 of this epistle).

not according to the covenant that I made with their fathers in the day when I took them by the hand to lead them out of the land of Egypt; because they did not continue in My covenant, and I disregarded them, says the LORD. When God rescued the Israelites from their enslavement in Egypt, God made a covenant with them according to the blood of animals (Ex. 25:8).

8:10 For this is the covenant that I will make with the house of Israel after those days, says the LORD: I will put My laws in their mind and write them on their hearts. The old covenant was written on two tablets of stone, then when Moses descended from the mountain, he found people worshipping the golden calf. God wrote it on stones as an indication that the peoples' hearts in the Old Testament were like stones. In the New Testament, however, God changed our nature and gave us, as the prophet Ezekiel says, *"a new heart and ... a new spirit"*; *"I will take the heart of stone out of your flesh and give you a heart of flesh"* (Ezek.

36:26). The word of God is written by the Holy Spirit on our hearts rather than on stone. When the word of God is thus written on our hearts and in our minds, it will transform us. For that reason, we will be enabled to maintain the commandments of God, due to this new nature we received from baptism.

and I will be their God, and they shall be My people. This is the same formula used to express all the covenants, beginning with Adam and carried out through the end of ages. God wants us to choose Him as our God, and in return, we would become His people. Hence, this basic core message resides in every covenant, and thus, has never changed throughout the ages; the only difference is that with each covenant God made, the set of principles surrounding them changed (for more, see discussion in commentary on Heb. 8:6).

8:11 None of them shall teach his neighbor, and none his brother, saying, "Know the LORD,' for all shall know Me. Does this mean that teaching in the New Testament is prohibited? Of course not. In the Old Testament, I could not go to God directly, because there was always a veil separating the people from God (*"The veil shall be a divider for you between the holy place and the Most Holy."*—Ex. 26:33). For that reason, there needed to be a mediator between God and us, which was usually the role taken on by the high priests or the prophets; however, there was hardly any direct communication between God and each of His people, simply because the way to the Holy of Holies was closed. St. Paul began this epistle saying, *"God, who at various times and in various ways spoke in time past to the fathers by the prophets, has in these last days spoken to us by His Son"* (Heb 1:1-2). This verse does not prohibit teaching, but simply emphasizes the personal relationship with Christ that each of us is allowed to have now, because now we can be united with Christ in a very personal way: in baptism, you put on Christ; in Chrismation, you become a tabernacle and Temple of God and the Holy Spirit abides in you; in Communion, you unite with Christ (as He said, *"He who eats My flesh and drinks My blood abides in Me, and I in him."*—John 6:56). Now there is available for each us a personal relationship between us and Christ. Hence, recognize the fact that the Temple of the Old Testament was not called a "house of prayer." It used to be called a *"house of sacrifice,"* as God pronounced to Solomon when He appeared to him, saying: *"I have heard your prayer, and have chosen this place for Myself as a house of sacrifice"* (2 Chr. 7:12). That is why in the Litany of the Assemblies, the priest says: *"houses of prayer, houses of purity, houses of blessing."* What is the difference? In the old covenant, when you enter into the Tabernacle of Meeting, the first thing you would confront was the altar of burnt offering. Hence, the first step was to offer a sacrifice. After offering such sacrifice, then you can enter into the Holy, which is where you would find the altar of incense, which symbolizes prayer. Hence, in a sense, you cannot offer prayer before God unless you have offered a sacrifice. But now, since Jesus Christ offered Himself as a sacrifice *"once for all"* (Rom. 6:10; Heb. 7:27, 9:12, 10:10), we can stand before God, raise our eyes to heaven, and lift our voice and call out to Him *"Abba"* (Rom. 8:15) and say, *"Our Father in heaven, hallowed be Your name, ... etc."*—*"And because you are sons, God has sent forth the Spirit of His Son into your hearts, crying out, 'Abba, Father!'"* (Gal. 4:6). (Note that Christ Himself referred to the Father in the same manner: *"And He said, 'Abba, Father, all things are possible for You'"* [Mark 14:36]). There is no longer any barrier between us and God. We no longer have to offer sacrifices first as in the old covenant. Now, there is a personal relationship with the Lord.

from the least of them to the greatest of them. From this portion of the verse, we can extract the principle that infant baptism—baptism of children—is an appropriate practice. God did not say *"only the adults will know Me."* Rather, He said, *"from the least of them to the greatest of them"*; hence everyone, from child to adult, is granted the opportunity to be baptized into Christ. The covenant is open to everyone, including children, as Christ said, *"Let the little children come to Me, and do not forbid them; for of such is the kingdom of heaven"* (Matt. 19:14).

8:12 For I will be merciful to their unrighteousness, and their sins and their lawless deeds I will remember no more. In the old covenant, as explained previously, a person's status began as that of a sinner, and in order to become righteous, a person must follow and maintain all the precepts in the law. However, once a single commandment was transgressed, that person would have been guilty of the entire law. In the New Testament, the blood of Christ has cleansed us completely from the beginning through baptism, as St. John tells us: *"The blood of Jesus Christ His Son cleanses us from all sin"* (1 John 1:7). That is why in the new covenant, our lawless deeds are forgiven because the blood of the Lamb, every day on the altar, has already been shed for us and in that blood we can whiten our clothes and become righteous again.

8:13 In that He says, "A new covenant," He has made the first obsolete. This in no way means that the new covenant has made the Old Testament Scriptures obsolete. If this was the case, then St. Paul would not be quoting from the Old Testament (as he quoted four verses from Jeremiah) as a means of supporting and elaborating upon his argument. St. Paul refers to this relationship as the covenant between God and man which was based on the righteousness of man rather than the righteousness of Christ. That covenant has been made obsolete. This word *"obsolete"* can also be regarded as referring to the Levitical priesthood and the sacrificial system of the earthly tabernacle.

Now what is becoming obsolete and growing old is ready to vanish away. Now, our relationship with God, which is founded on the three principles set forth in verses 10, 11, and 12, have displaced the former relationship we once had with Him.

Chapter 8 Questions

1. In what sense is Jesus Christ the "Mediator" of a new covenant? What did He do to mediate?

2. What are the stages of the covenant?

3. Why did the old covenant fail?

4. What are the primary promises of the new covenant as prophesied in Jeremiah 31:31-34?

5. What was made obsolete by the new covenant?

9

Chapter Outline

- The Tabernacle (1-5)
- Worship in the Tabernacle (6-10)
- Christ entered by His own blood (11-14)
- The Mediator of a new covenant (15-28)

Introduction

St. Paul argued previously that the new covenant is superior to the old covenant because Christ, the true High Priest, serves in the heavenly sanctuary rather than merely the earthly one, which was a copy and shadow of the heavenly. Now, in Chapter 9, in order to prove further the excellence of the new covenant, St. Paul compared between two things: the place and manner of worship in the New Testament as compared with the Old Testament. He will explain in this chapter that, while the old manner and place of worship inhibited people's access to God, in the new sanctuary, the door is open and we have direct access to God. For this reason, a rough diagram of the tabernacle is provided below.

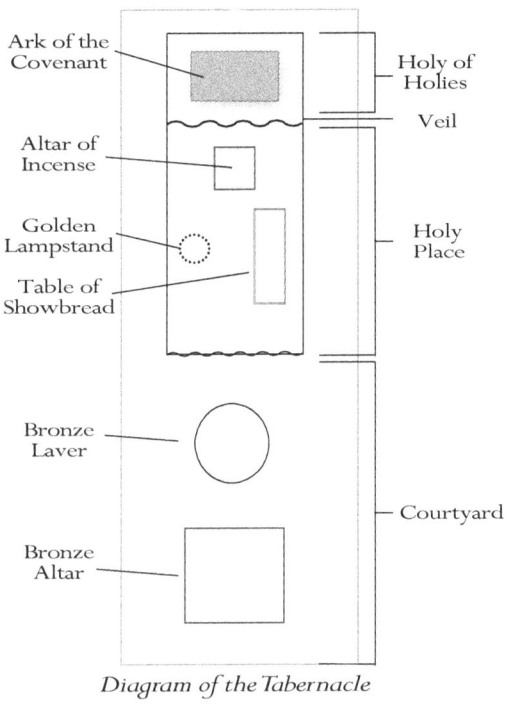

Diagram of the Tabernacle

9:1 Then indeed, even the first covenant had. St. Paul is saying that the old covenant had two things:

ordinances of divine service. This refers to the rituals they maintained in the Old Testament, such as offering of sacrifices and atoning for people's sins.

and the earthly sanctuary. This refers to the physical structure in which worship took place: the Tabernacle of Meeting, whose structure will be explained by St. Paul in the ensuing verses.

9:2 For a tabernacle was prepared: the first part, in which was the lampstand, the table, and the showbread, which is called the sanctuary. *"The first part"* refers to the section of the tabernacle referred to as the sanctuary or, more commonly, the *"Holy Place"* (Ex. 26:33), where you will find three things: as you enter that section, on your right, you would find the table of showbread; on your left would be the golden lampstand, and in front of you, just before passing the veil and entering into the next part of the tabernacle, you would find the altar of incense.

9:3 and behind the second veil. St. Paul considered the entrance to the Holy Place to be like the first veil, while the veil separating the Holy Place from the Holy of Holies was referred to by him as the *"second veil."*

the part of the tabernacle which is called the Holiest of All. The literal translation of the Hebrew idiom which is intended to express this portion of the tabernacle is *"Holy of Holies."* In modern biblical translations, such as the New King James Version, they opted for a less literal translation and described it here as *"Holiest of All"* and elsewhere as the *"Most Holy"* (e.g., Exodus 26:33).

9:4-5 In the Holy of Holies was the Ark of the Covenant, inside of which were three things: the golden pot which had the manna that fell from heaven, Aaron's rod that budded, and the tablets of the covenant, and on top of which was a cover called the mercy seat, The ark of the covenant had a cover that was made of pure gold, which was called the *"mercy seat."* On this mercy seat, two cherubim overshadowed it. Below you will find a discussion of each of those things.

which had the golden censer. We know the altar of incense to have been just outside the veil that leads you to the Holy of Holies. What about the golden censer, which we read here is inside the Holy of Holies, but is usually kept outside with the altar of incense? Is the golden censer inside or outside the veil? And if so, is there a contradiction here? No. In the ritual of the Day of Atonement, upon which St. Paul focuses in this chapter, the priest used to take the golden censer with its incense in it and enter into the Holy of Holies (Lev. 16:12-13).

Of these things we cannot now speak in detail. Although St. Paul did not mention an explanation for all of these things, but this verse is very important. It indicates that St. Paul considered that there was a deep meaning underlying everything in the Tabernacle of Meeting. Actually, in order to understand the church structure and layout, Christ's sacrifice, and also the Divine Liturgy, a person needs to study and understand the structure of the Tabernacle of Meeting as well as the sacrifice of the Old Testament. At this point, since St. Paul was unable to provide us more detail in his epistle, but I will share with you some symbolism regarding the Tabernacle of Meeting.

✤ *The lampstand* ~ The lampstand was made of gold, which symbolizes her purity. It also carried light, also symbolizing St. Mary in that she carried the True Light in her womb.

✤ *The manna pot* ~ With regard to the manna pot, it was likewise made of gold, again symbolizing her purity. Additionally, the manna was the bread that fell from heaven and sustained the children of Israel in the wilderness of Sinai, which symbolizes the Lord Jesus Christ. Hence, the golden manna pot that carried the manna symbolizes the pure St. Mary who carried the Lord Christ, the Bread of Life (see John 6 in which He speaks of Himself as the manna that fell from heaven).

✤ *The golden censer* ~ The golden censer again symbolizes St. Mary in the following ways: the gold, her purity, the incense and sweet aroma symbolizes the Lord Christ in her womb (recall that the Bible speaks of the Father having smelled the "sweet-smelling aroma" of Christ's sacrifice on the cross—Eph. 5:2).

✤ *Aaron's Rod* ~ Aaron's rod, which sprouted blossoms and ripe almonds (Num. 17:8) without planting or watering, likewise symbolizes St. Mary because, without the seed of man, she gave birth to Christ.

✤ *Ark of the Covenant* ~ The Ark of the Covenant can also be said to symbolize St. Mary, since she, being clothed with purity (as the Ark is overlaid with gold), carried inside her body the Lord Christ (who is symbolized by the contents of the Ark). This is why in the icon of Saint Mary you find two angels overshadowing her, referencing the two cherubim that are overshadowing the mercy seat above the Ark. Moreover, aside from the previous mention of those things that symbolize Christ above—that is, the light, the bread, the sweet aroma of incense, and what sprouted out of Aaron's rod—the Ark of the Covenant also symbolizes Christ. It was made of wood, which was overlaid with gold from within and without. The wood symbolizes the humanity of our Lord Jesus Christ, while the gold symbolizes His divinity. Inside the ark, among other things, a person would have found the two tablets of the covenant, which are the word of God. Christ is the Logos—the Word.

✤ *The mercy seat* ~ The cover of the Ark of the covenant, which was called the mercy seat, had two cherubim stretching their wings above it, "covering the mercy seat with their wings," facing one another (Ex. 25:20). This symbolizes the throne of

God, because God used to appear and speak to Aaron and Moses from the mercy seat. This also symbolizes God because He is seated in heaven upon the cherubim and is surrounded by myriads of angels who worship Him incessantly.

9:6-7 Now when these things had been thus prepared. In other words, after the Tabernacle of Meeting was prepared according to the pattern shown to Moses by God.

the priests ... went into the first part of the tabernacle ... But into the second part the high priest went alone. Here St. Paul starts to compare the Holy, which is called here *"the first part of the tabernacle,"* and the Holy of the Holies, which was behind the veil. The first difference is that in the Holy, all priests were allowed to enter, but in the Holy of Holies, only the high priest.

always ... performing the services, But into the second part the high priest went ... once a year. The second difference between the Holy and the Holy of Holies (as is explained in Ex. 27:20-21, 30:7-8; and Lev. 24:5-9) is that in the Holy, priests used to enter it on a daily basis to offer incense, to light the lampstand, to change the bread on the Table of Showbread, etc. Hence, morning through evening, every single day, priests preformed various services in the Holy, while in the Holy of Holies, only on a single day was there any ritual performed.

not without blood. Why are our sins covered by blood? Because *"the wages of sin is death"* (Rom. 6:23). Shedding of blood means the sin has been punished. That is why the high priest cannot enter into the Holy of Holies on the Day of Atonement without blood.

which he offered for himself and for the people's sins. Because the high priest, as previously mentioned, was a normal human who was sinful, so therefore, he had to offer a sacrifice for himself as well as for the people. This was not the case for the true High Priest, Christ, who had no sin: *"For such a High Priest was fitting for us, who is holy, harmless, undefiled, separate from sinners, and has become higher than the heavens"* (Heb. 7:26).

committed in ignorance. As mentioned previously (in commentary on Heb. 5:2), this is a reference to Numbers 15:27-31, in which the Lord asked the priests to offer a sacrifice for sins committed in ignorance, but the sins that were committed willingly and were accompanied by a rejection of the authority of God during the rest of the person's life, for them there was no such offering. Hence, St. Paul here is giving them a hint related to his general theme: apostasy is not a sin committed in ignorance, but rather involves people who know the Old Testament very well, who accepted Christ, who (as explained previously in the commentary on Heb. 6:4-8) were already partakers of the Holy Spirit and had tasted the heavenly gift, then now if they commit the sin of apostasy, they are doing this willingly and therefore, it cannot be forgiven. Every sin can be forgiven, but as explained in the commentary about Chapter 6 of this epistle, it is practically impossible for an apostate to repent and therefore will in all practical likelihood cause themselves to be rejected for choosing to reject the Lord Christ.

Summary

✞ Rituals on Day of Atonement ✞

Only the high priest was allowed to enter into the Holy of Holies, only once a year, and such entry required the shedding the blood of animals.

That one day on which the high priest entered into the Holy of Holies was called the Day of Atonement. Atonement means reconciliation or to be united as one with God; but this word does not accurately reflect the Hebrew term for this word (יום כיפור), which is transliterated Yom Kippur. This word can be literally translated as meaning "to cover." Hence, the Day of Atonement refers to covering people's sins. In the New Testament, by Christ's blood, our sins were covered and therefore, we are reconciled with God through Him, being able to become united with God. The rituals of this day are summarized as follows:

- First, the high priest offers a bull for his own sins.

- He then takes a censer full of coals and incense from the altar of incense and enters into the Holy of Holies (as explained previously).

- Then the priest sprinkles the blood of the bull on the mercy seat of the ark.

- For the sins of the people, the priest offers a goat as a sin offering.

- He takes the blood of the goat and sprinkles it on the mercy seat.

- Then, he makes atonement for the altar itself with the blood of both the bull and the goat on the horns of the altar.

- Afterward, another goat, which had been designated as the *"scapegoat"* (Lev. 16:8, 10, 16), would be sent away alive into the wilderness, bearing the sins of the people. This scapegoat has many beautiful meanings:

  o It symbolizes the departure of sin from the

camp of Israel, because it carried all the sins of the people and then was sent to the wilderness.

o It also symbolized the Lord Jesus Christ who carried our sins. By offering one goat as a sin offering and allowing it to die on behalf of the people, and then sending another goat away alive, you can see how this signifies Christ who was both crucified and also resurrected.

- After all of this, the high priest offers a burnt offering for himself and for the people for the purpose of sending up a sweet aroma to God (*"And the priest shall burn all on the altar as a burnt sacrifice, an offering made by fire, a sweet aroma to the LORD."*—Lev. 1:9). This symbolizes, of course, Christ's death which was regarded as an offering of a sweet aroma to God the Father, as St. Paul says elsewhere: *"Christ also has loved us and given Himself for us, an offering and a sacrifice to God for a sweet-smelling aroma"* (Eph. 5:2).

9:8 the Holy Spirit indicating this. There are two important lessons from these words. First, the Holy Spirit inspired the writers of the Old Testament to write down the things we find written there for us. Second, when we read the Bible, the Holy Spirit continues to speak to us through the word of the Bible. Hence, the Holy Spirit did not simply inspire the authors of the different writings in the Bible and then His mission ceased, but rather, His work continues every single time we read the word of God. That why is St. Paul said *"indicating"* in the present, continuing sense.

that the way into the Holiest of All was not yet made manifest. The way into the Holy of Holies was not yet revealed—in other words, there was still restricted access to God during the Old Testament. Why this restricted access? Because it is only the high priest who enters, not everyone; also, he enters only once a year; additionally, he must enter with blood for atonement; moreover, this has to happen every year, and thus, this sacrifice is not sufficient to accomplish forgiveness once for all (as was Christ's sacrifice—see Rom. 6:20; Heb. 7:27, 9:12, 10:10). Hence, the sacrifices offered on the Day of Atonement were deficient; otherwise, they would not need to be repeated every year.

while the first tabernacle was still standing. This can be understood in two ways: as long as the Holy stands and the Holy of the Holies remains separated by a veil, then access to the Holy of Holies remains blocked. Another way to understand this is that, as long as the rituals of the Old Testament (including the Levitical priesthood and the sacrifices they were required to perform) continued to exist, then the way to the true tabernacle in heaven is blocked. That is why, around the time when the Lord Jesus Christ offered Himself as a sacrifice on the cross, two things happened: first, the veil was torn apart in two from top to bottom (Matt. 27:51; Mark 15:38; Luke 23:45), signifying that the first tabernacle is obsolete; second, the high priest, during the trial of Christ, *"tore his clothes"* (Matt. 26:65; Mark 14:63), signifying the end of the era and need for Levitical priesthood.

9:9 It was symbolic for the present time in which both gifts and sacrifices are offered which cannot make him who performed the service perfect in regard to the conscience. St. Paul is saying that the worship in the old covenant was symbolic. The way to God the Father was blocked by our sins. But now, through the sacrifice of Christ, the door to heaven has been opened for us. The symbols of the old covenant could not make the worshippers (*"who performed the service"* indirectly through the priest) perfect. The system of the Old Testament was not only deficient, but it could not "perfect in regard to the conscience." In our minds, the conscience usually refers to the sense inside us that differentiates between right and wrong; but St. Paul speaks about the conscience in a different way here, referring to the part of our thoughts that retains and remembers our former sins, which rebukes us. If these sacrifices forgave us truly, our conscience would not rebuke us in this way. The sacrifices in the Old Testament did not truly forgive people's sins, but served as a symbol of forgiveness. That is why all the fathers in the Old Testament went to Hades until Christ was crucified and then transferred them into Paradise. It was a promise of future forgiveness, and therefore their conscience could not be made truly perfect, forgetting one's past sins, which were like the veil separating them from God. That is why a sacrifice had to be repeated every year, because one's conscience was not made perfect.

9:10 concerned only with foods and drinks, various washings, and fleshly ordinances. In this verse, St. Paul is saying that the rituals of the Old Testament were simply external. They provided temporary help, allowing for outward cleansing (that is why it is called here *"fleshly ordinances"*). But such rituals did not affect one's internal need for cleansing. The conscience was made perfect. Maybe from the outside people looked like they were clean and ready to worship, but in actuality, their spirits still awaited true atonement.

imposed until the time of reformation. The rituals of the Old Testament were given as a means of temporary assistance, awaiting the time of the incarnation of the Son of God, His crucifixion, resurrection, and the start of the new covenant and priesthood of Jesus Christ.

9:11-14 Now St. Paul will compare the ordinances of the Old Testament with those of the New. He is trying to portray the fact that Christ is a better priest, had a better ministry, served in a better sanctuary, and offered a better sacrifice. St. Paul also shows that Christ's blood served three main functions: atonement (covering our sins), redemption (setting us free by ransom of His blood), and sanctification (purifying us to be in communion with God).

9:11 But Christ came as High Priest of the good things to come. This is the first difference mentioned by St. Paul, comparing between the priesthood of the Old Testament and Christ's high priesthood in the New. The priesthood of Christ offered *"good things to come."* Actually, according to other translations of the Bible, this is translated as *"good things that have come."* These good things refer to the open access to heaven, being able to stand and call to God as being our Father in heaven. Priesthood in the old covenant provided restricted access, while the priesthood of the new covenant provided open access to God.

with the greater and more perfect tabernacle not made with hands, that is, not of this creation. The second aspect of St. Paul's comparison is the sanctuary. The sanctuary of the old covenant was man-made, but the sanctuary of the new covenant—heaven—was not made by man's hands, but is greater and better in that it was God Himself who made it.

9:12 Not with the blood of goats and calves, but with His own blood. The third comparison given by St. Paul is regarding sacrifices. In the Old Testament, the sacrifices involved animals, but in the New Testament, the sacrifice which atones our sins involves the shedding of Christ's own blood.

He entered the Most Holy Place once for all. The fourth point of comparison by St. Paul relates to the frequency of the sacrifice for the atonement of sins. In the old covenant, as discussed previously, sacrifices were required every year, but in the new covenant, we have received Christ's sacrifice once for all. And as explained previously in this commentary, this word, *"all,"* can refer to two things. Christ offered Himself once for all people, and it can also refer to the notion that Christ offered Himself once for all time.

having obtained eternal redemption. The fifth difference between the old and new covenants that St. Paul describes involves the notion that sacrifices in the Old Testament served merely as a temporary promise of forgiveness, but in the New Testament, by Christ's sacrifice, we have access to *"eternal redemption."*

	OLD COVENANT	NEW COVENANT
Priesthood	Restricted access	"good things to come": access to God
Sanctuary	Man-made, earthly temple	Greater and perfect sanctuary in heaven; God's own presence
Sacrifices	The blood of goats and calves	Christ's own blood
Frequency	Every year	Once for all
Forgiveness	Temporary forgiveness	Eternal redemption

redemption. St. Paul used a term here he did not use before in this epistle. Previously he used the word *"atonement"* whose meaning was explained previously (see "Rituals on Day of Atonement" after commentary on Heb. 9:6-7). Redemption refers to setting a slave free for a ransom (a purchase price) (for more, see Lev. 25; Num. 3). Hence, when St. Paul said *"eternal redemption,"* he is saying that our freedom from the slavery of sin and the Devil was purchased by the blood of our Lord Jesus Christ. Hence, there was a *"ransom"* here, which is a word used by St. Paul in his first letter to Timothy (*"who gave Himself a ransom for all, to be testified in due time."*—1 Tim. 2:6); this word was also used by the Lord Christ to refer to His sacrifice (*"The Son of Man did not come to be served, but to serve, and to give His life a ransom for many."*—Matt. 20:28; Mark 10:45). I am emphasizing this word *"ransom"* because some contemporary theologians, unfortunately, refuse to describe Christ's sacrifice in this way, that Christ purchased us by His blood to redeem us as if we were slaves that needed redemption money to be set free. Hence, the blood of Christ did not only atone for our sins, but by the shedding of His blood all those who follow Him are set free from the slavery of sin and wickedness.

9:13 **For if the blood of bulls and goats and the ashes of a heifer, sprinkling the unclean, sanctifies for the purifying of the flesh.** St. Paul is referring to both the Day of Atonement (involving the *"blood of bulls and goats"*) and also another ritual aside from the Day of Atonement, which involves the sprinkling of the ashes of a heifer. This second ritual refers to the rites regarding the *"red heifer"* mentioned in Numbers Chapter 19. Let me summarize the ritual of the red heifer. They would take a red heifer without defect or blemish that had never been under yoke, and it was to be slaughtered outside the camp. Then the carcass would be completely burned with cedar wood, hyssop, and read thread. After the heifer was completely burned with cedar wood, hyssop, and red thread, its ashes were gathered and stored to be combined with water for use in ceremonies of purification. So, for example, if anyone became unclean and therefore defiled by touching a dead body, they were to be purified by sprinkling a mixture of these ashes from the red heifer and water over such a person. That is what St. Paul referred to the *"ashes of a heifer."*

9:14 how much more shall the blood of Christ, who ... offered Himself without spot to God. In the previous verse, St. Paul tells us that anyone who was unclean due to touching a dead body was purified through the ashes derived from the ritual of the red heifer. This ritual simply purified the flesh—the external man—rather than the conscience of a person. St. Paul now, in this verse, utilizes the meaning of the word *"purification"* to explain the benefits of the blood shed by the Lord Christ, comparing between the purification of the old and new covenants. (Note that the word *"purification"* can be understood to signify the term *"sanctification"*—see Heb. 10:10) The red heifer symbolized Christ. St. Paul discusses three main differences between the purification of the Old Testament with that of the New Testament.

cleanse your conscience. (1) of 3. In the Levitical system, the ritual of the red heifer simply purified the external flesh, while the sacrifice of Christ has the power to purify our internal conscience.

from dead works. (2) of 3. The Levitical system purified defilement that was contracted passively (by simply coming into contact with that which was impure), but Christ's blood purifies our conscience from dead works, which refers to the active violations of the will of God..

to serve the living God. (3) of 3. Whereas the purification rituals in the Old Testament allowed for an impure person (who as a result of his impurity was sent out of the camp of the Israelites) to return and resume contact with his people, Christ's sacrifice provides the degree of purification that allows the believer to worship the living God.

who through the eternal Spirit. We say in the Coptic Psalmody (on Tuesday), *"For of His own will, the pleasure of His Father, and the Holy*

Spirit, He came and saved us." Hence, the sacrifice of Christ was by Christ's will, to the pleasure of His Father and also the pleasure of the Holy Spirit. The word "eternal Spirit" refers to the notion that the crucifixion of Christ was not an accident, but it was a voluntary sacrifice which God planned to offer long before His death on the cross. That is why Christ said, *"Therefore My Father loves Me, because I lay down My life that I may take it again. No one takes it from Me, but I lay it down of Myself. I have power to lay it down, and I have power to take it again. This command I have received from My Father"* (John 10:17-18). The death of Christ was not involuntary, as is the death of virtually all human beings; rather, it was voluntary, to the pleasure of the Father and the Holy Spirit.

9:15 And for this reason He is the Mediator of the new covenant. St. Paul begins now to explain why Christ is the Mediator of the new covenant. It is because the new covenant offered all the things mentioned above: atonement, redemption, and sanctification, which the Old Testament was incapable of sufficiently offering.

by means of death. How did Christ become the Mediator of the new covenant? By offering Himself as a sacrifice.

for the redemption of the transgressions under the first covenant. There was a covenant between God and us in the Old Testament (for more on the term *"covenant"* see commentary on Heb. 6, *"inasmuch as He is also a Mediator"*). According to this covenant, any transgression was to be punished by death. Thus, in order for Christ to redeem us due to the *"transgressions under the first covenant,"* He offered Himself on the cross as a sacrifice on our behalf. By dying on the cross, He became a Mediator of the new covenant.

that those who are called. Who are *"those?"* Everyone is called, but attaining the benefits of Christ's redemptive act depends on whether we accept that calling. It is those who accept Christ's calling that are referred to here among *"those who are called."* Rejecting the calling of Christ means you will not be counted among *"those who are called"* who "receive the promise of eternal inheritance."

may receive the promise of the eternal inheritance. The result of the shedding of Christ's blood, which allowed us to receive atonement, redemption, and sanctification, is that all the participants in the new covenant may enjoy the benefit of eternal inheritance.

9:16-17 testament. The Greek

word translated here as *"testament"* is διαθήκη, transliterated diathēkē, which is in almost all instances in the NKJV translated as *"covenant,"* and in other translations, this word in this particular verse is appropriately translated as *"covenant."* According to the New American Standard Bible version, verses 16-17 are translated as follows: *"For where a covenant is, there must of necessity be the death of the one who made it. For a covenant is valid only when men are dead, for it is never in force while the one who made it lives."*

For where there is a testament, there must also of necessity be the death of the testator. For a testament is in force after men are dead, since it has no power at all while the testator lives. St. Paul is here referring to a very well known ritual regarding entering into a covenant with another party (which is very different from a simple contract as is common these days; See commentary on Heb. 6, *"inasmuch as He is also a Mediator"*). Briefly, to explain the term covenant, in Genesis 15, we can see that both parties who enter into a covenant walk down a path of blood belonging to an animal, whose body is cut in two with each part of the body laid on either side of the path, signifying that anyone who breaks the covenant is subject to death. Thus, the death of this animal symbolizes the death of the person who makes the covenant (the *"testator"*); as the sacrifice died, also too the person who breaks the covenant will suffer the penalty of death. Hence, without this ritual involving the notion of death, then the covenant has no effect. This covenant is in force and effective after the slaying of the animal, which symbolizes the death of anyone who enters into and breaks the covenant.

9:18 Therefore not even the first covenant was dedicated without blood. St. Paul is saying, for any covenant to be effective, there has to the shedding of blood. Blood symbolizes life (as the Bible says, *"the life of the flesh is in the blood"*—Lev. 17:11). Shedding of blood symbolizes the price of breaking a covenant, which is death. The old covenant was dedicated with blood. Here, St. Paul is implicitly making reference to a very well known story in the Old Testament, which he explains in the next set of verses.

9:19 For when Moses had spoken every precept to all the people according to the law, he took the blood of calves and goats, with water, scarlet wool, and hyssop, and sprinkled both the book itself and all the people. In the Old Testament, Moses took the blood of animals and sprinkled this blood on the book of the covenants as well as all the people. Why? So that this covenant would be effective, because without the shedding of blood, this covenant is without any real practical effect.

9:20 saying, "This is the blood of the covenant which God has commanded you." The old covenant was expressed by those words, and likewise in the New Testament, Jesus Christ, during the Mystical Supper, at which time He gave His blood to His disciples, did so while saying, *"This is My blood of the new covenant, which is shed for many for the remission of sins"* (Matt. 26:28).

9:21 Then likewise he sprinkled with blood both the tabernacle and all the vessels of the ministry. Moses did not only sprinkle the book of the covenant and the people, but also the tabernacle, the vessels, and the altar.

9:22 And according to the law almost all things are purified with blood, and without shedding of blood there is no remission. Why is everything purified with blood? As explained previously, blood stands for life, and the forgiveness of sin costs life itself, for the *"wages of sin is death"* (Rom. 6:23). So, God gives the life of His own son to show us the depth of His love when He forgives us our sins. Many people wonder why Christ had to die on the cross, and why He could not just have forgiven people by the word of His mouth. Here in this verse and in the preceding verses, St. Paul explains that the shedding of the blood of Christ was a must, as He is the one who entered into a covenant with us (but He was the only person who walked down the blood path, signifying that He is the only one who could die on behalf of our sins when the covenant was broken—for more, see commentary on Heb. 8:6, *"inasmuch as He is also a Mediator"*).

9:23-26 In this set of verses, it is as if St. Paul was returning to the same themes that He discussed in the beginning of this chapter from verse 1-14 (and also elsewhere in the epistle, particularly Chapter 8).

9:23 Therefore it was necessary that the copies of the things in the heavens should be purified with these, but the heavenly things themselves with better sacrifices than these. The Tabernacle of Meeting was a shadow and a copy of the things in heaven (see Heb. 9:21; also see Heb. 8:2 and 8:5). Christ's sacrifice, symbolized in many of the Old Testament rituals, was the ultimate and superior sacrifice to which all of the ones in the Old Testament pointed.

9:24 **For Christ has not entered the holy places made with hands, which are copies of the true, but into heaven itself, now to appear in the presence of God for us.** Christ entered into the true heavenly sanctuary, unlike the priests who entered the Holy and the high priest who alone entered the Holy of Holies, both of which were part of a tabernacle made by hands, whereas heaven was created by God (see Heb. 8:2 and 9:2 for more). The heavenly sanctuary is where we find the real presence of God, rather than in the earthly one.

9:25 **not that He should offer Himself often, as the high priest enters the Most Holy Place every year with blood of another.** The high priest enters the Most Holy Place—the Holy of Holies—not with the shedding of his own blood but by shedding the blood of animals. Christ, on the other hand, shed His own blood to bestow atonement upon all of us. (For more, see Heb. 9:6-7).

9:26 **He then would have had to suffer often since the foundation of the world; but now, once at the end of the ages, He has appeared to put away sin by the sacrifice of Himself.** If the Lord Christ had to offer Himself often, on a regular basis (like the sacrifices that were offered according to the old covenant), then Christ would have also suffered often. But Christ suffered only once, and therefore died once for all *"at the end of ages"* (which means at the *"fullness of the time"* [Gal. 4:4]—at just the right time) (see also Heb. 9:6-7 and 9:12). Christ carried the burden and sin of humanity on Himself, and then offered Himself as a sin sacrifice on the cross, to atone for our sins, redeeming us and allowing for our sanctification once for all time and for all people (who will receive the benefits of the salvation Christ accomplished for them if they accept His calling).

9:27-28 **And as it is appointed for men to die once, but after this the judgment, so Christ was offered once to bear the sins of many. To those who eagerly wait for Him.** For all of us, after each of us die, we will be reserved for judgment. Christ died once in order to carry our judgment in His body by carrying our sins. When He comes in His Second Coming, He will come for salvation to those who believe in Him and followed Him, eagerly waiting for Him. Notice here that St. Paul does not say *"sins of all,"* but rather, *"sins of many,"* because not everyone will accept Christ and therefore, those who do not accept Him will not receive the blessings of His life-giving blood. He called everyone and died for all, but only those who respond to His call to them will gain the benefits of His blood.

He will appear a second time, apart from sin, for salvation. Christ will not appear again as He did during His First Coming, at which time He appeared to bear the sins of many as a sin offering on behalf of humanity, as *"the lamb of God who takes away the sin of the world"* (as He was introduced at the start of His ministry by St. John the Baptist in John 1:29). During His Second Coming, Christ will come for salvation, not as a sin offering. He will come bringing salvation to those who eagerly await Him. Thus, He did once—the first time—to bear the sins of many; He will return once more—the second time He comes—for the purpose of salvation.

Chapter 9 Questions

1. What are the three main effects of the Lord's sacrifice? Explain the difference.

2. In what way does Christ's sacrifice of Himself cleanse the conscience in a way that the animal sacrifices of the old covenant could not?

3. What is required for forgiveness to be granted?

4. Read Hebrews 9:15 and 1 Timothy 2:5. In what sense does Jesus serve as a Mediator?

5. How does the purpose of Christ's First Coming differ from His Second Coming?

10

Chapter Outline

- Ineffectiveness of the Levitical system (1-5)
- Sanctification through Christ's sacrifice (5-10)
- Christ, the new High Priest (11-14)
- The adequacy of the new covenant (15-18)
- Call to use our access to God (19-25)
- Fourth warning: the danger of shrinking back (26-31)

Introduction

In all the previous chapters, St. Paul gave proof for the superiority of Christ's ministry and His work. Now, St. Paul will shift to addressing what is accomplished in the life of the believers as a result of what Christ has done. We know that Christ's sacrifice allowed us access to God, among the many other blessings mentioned in the previous chapters of this epistle. But how does this affect my life, and why is it important to me personally? The main point that St. Paul will try to impress on us is the notion that by Christ our conscience can be cleansed. Before Christ, I retained a consciousness of sin—a recollection of sin, regardless of sacrifices aimed at the atonement of sin; but through Christ, we can clear our conscience from past sins. The Levitical system failed in cleansing us from sin and creating a clear conscience within us, but the ministry of Christ succeeded where the Levitical system failed.

10:1-4 This set of verses focuses on how the Levitical system was ineffective in clearing our conscience from sin.

10:1 For the law, having a shadow of the good things to come, and not the very image of the things, can never with these same sacrifices, which they offer continually year by year, make those who approach perfect. The Levitical system cannot perfect those who approach God, making them perfect. Why? He gave two reasons. First, it is the shadow and not the very image of the thing (as mentioned previously in the commentary—see Heb. 8:2 and 8:5). Because it is merely a copy and shadow of the reality—who is Christ—*"which they offer continually year by year,"* it cannot *"make those who approach perfect."* St. Paul emphasizes here again (as he did in previous parts of this epistle), the fact that it is done every year with the same sort of sacrifices (e.g., sin sacrifice, trespass sacrifice, etc.), and the fact that it is repeated by the priests and the high priest, then this means the Levitical system was deficient in allowing us access to God. The second reason is mentioned in verse 4 below (see commentary on Heb. 10:4).

10:2 **For then would they not have ceased to be offered? For the worshipers, once purified, would have had no more consciousness of sins.** If the Levitical system was adequate, then the sacrifices that were being offered should have been sufficient to have occurred once to accomplish their intended purpose. But the fact that the offerings were repeated yearly (and even daily for certain offerings) indicated a deficiency in the system. If people were truly purified by these sacrifices, the people would have had *"no more consciousness of sins."* However, since these offerings were repeated, it means that they were not adequate in achieving purification.

10:3 **But in those sacrifices there is a reminder of sins every year.** Every year, in the Old Testament, both God and us remembered our sins. When we offer sacrifices every year on the Day of Atonement (see Heb. 9:6-7 for more), we know that our sins are not forgiven, which is why we have to offer the sacrifices ever year. Since such sacrifices were inadequate in atoning sin, then God remembered the sins as well and held them against us.

10:4 **For it is not possible that the blood of bulls and goats could take away sins.** This is the second of two reasons (see Heb. 10:1) for why the Levitical system cannot perfect those who want to approach God. Usually, only the sacrifice of the greater for the lesser is adequate, not the opposite. Christ is greater, and we are lesser than Him, so when He offered Himself as a sacrifice for us, His offering was adequate to cleanse us from our sins. But the opposite is not possible: the bulls and goats offered (and here St. Paul is referring to the Day of Atonement—see Heb. 9:6-7 for more on this subject) were lesser than the humans offering them, so they could not sufficiently take away people's sins

10:5-10 This set of verses addresses the solution to the problem stated in the last set of verses, which is: if the sacrifices according to the Levitical system were inadequate in allowing us to achieve purification and clearing our conscience, then what is adequate?

10:5-7 **Therefore, when He came into the world.** St. Paul speaks here about Christ's incarnation. Also, notice that the phrase *"He came into the world"* exhibits Christ's divine attribute of being eternal; if He came into the world, He had to have come from somewhere, and thus, He existed prior to His birth. St. Paul did not say, *"when He was born,"* but rather *"when He came into the world."* Hence, Christ is eternal and without a beginning as the Father is also without a beginning.

He said. St. Paul here is about the quote a prophecy about Christ from Psalm 40:6-8. St. Paul quotes here from the Septuagint translation, and for that reason you will find some variation from what you read here and what you read in the Psalms according to other translations of the Bible. Since the Septuagint was the basis for virtually all Old Testament quotations by the apostles and the Early Church Fathers, for that reason it is considered the authorized version of the Old Testament according to the Orthodox Church.

Sacrifice and offering You did not desire ... In burnt offerings and sacrifices for sin You had no pleasure. Here the Son (i.e., Christ) is talking to the Father. "You did not desire sacrifices, because if You did, You would have been happy with all the sacrifices that were offered for the forgiveness of sins. So, when You sent me to the world, I came not to offer the same sacrifices of the animals as before, but to offer another sacrifice." The next verse elaborates more on the sacrifice Christ would offer.

But a body You have prepared for Me. ... Then I said, "Behold, I have come—In the volume of the book it is written of Me—To do Your will, O God." This verse is not only about incarnation, regarding how *"the Word became flesh and dwelt among us"* (John 1:14). More than this, the verse quoted here refers to how the Father prepared for Christ a body to be offered as a sacrifice. "When I come into the world, I will not offer animal sacrifices like the Levitical priests, but You prepared for Me a body to be offered as a sacrifice instead. If this is Your will, then that I will do." There are three points then: first, "You do not want Me to offer animal sacrifices"; second, "Instead, You prepared a body for Me to offer as a sacrifice"; third, "If this is Your will, I will do it, as it is prophesied about Me in Scripture" (which is what the Lord said in the Garden of Gethsemane when He prayed, *"nevertheless, not what I will, but what You will"* [Mark 14:36; Luke 22:42]; and let me make clear that there is no contradiction between the will of the Father and that of the Son, but it is simply an expression of complete obedience of the Son to the Father; for more, see commentary on Heb. 5:7, *"and was heard"*). The will of God the Father, and therefore, also the Son, was our sanctification, not through animal sacrifices, but through the body of our Lord Jesus Christ. As the Son obeyed the Father to the point of His death on the cross (as St. Paul tells us in his epistle to the Philippians, *"He humbled Himself and became obedient to the point of death, even the death of the cross."*—Phil. 2:8), that is why we need to follow His example and be willing to obey the will of the Father even unto death, which is why we say in the Lord's prayer, *"Thy will be done."*

10:8-9 **Previously saying, "Sacrifice and offering, burnt offerings, and offerings for sin You did not desire, nor had pleasure in them" (which are offered according to the law), then He said, "Behold, I have come to do Your will, O God."** This reiterates what was mentioned in the previous set of verses (10:5-7). Notice the complete and utter obedience of Christ to the Father. This reminds us of what Samuel the prophet said to Saul: *"to obey is better than sacrifice, and to heed than the fat of rams"* (1 Sam. 15:22). And here I want to highlight a very important point. If I offer a sacrifice, but not with an obedient heart, it will not be accepted. What makes my sacrifice acceptable to God? It is the spirit of obedience. What made the sacrifice of Christ acceptable before God? Because He obeyed the Father. That is why obedience is more important than sacrifice, because without it, one's sacrifice is meaningless. Hence, as the Lord Jesus Christ obeyed, in the same way, in order for our sacrifices (e.g., a sacrifice of praise, prayer, offering our bodies in fasting and worshipping the Lord, etc.) to be accepted, they have to come from an obedient heart that willingly submits to the will of God.

He takes away the first that He may establish the second. The *"first"* refers to the Levitical system of animal sacrifices which was displaced by *"the second,"* which is the sacrifice of the Lord Jesus Christ. Hence, the old covenant was replaced by the new one. By being obedient to the will of the Father and foregoing animal sacrifice while substituting Himself as a sacrifice instead, Christ took away the Levitical system and old covenant, establishing in its stead the new covenant. Notice how the Old Testament itself attests to the deficiency of the Levitical system. The prophets were looking for a new covenant to atone our sins and clear our conscience.

10:10 **By that will we have been sanctified through the offering of the body of Jesus Christ once for all.** For the Lord Jesus Christ, the will of God included a sacrificial death for our sanctification.

offering of the body. Pay attention to St. Paul's focus on Christ's body and flesh, which He will discuss again one more time later in this chapter (in v. 20). He has already mentioned it once before when speaking of how the Father prepared a body for Christ to sacrifice (Heb. 10:5). The Son offered this body on the cross because this is the will of the Father.

10:11-14 Now, from verse 11 to 14, St. Paul will again reflect on the priesthood of Christ: Christ as the new High Priest. Every time St. Paul mentions this subject, he adds something new regarding the superiority of the priesthood of Christ over Levitical priesthood. The last point he reached in Chapter 9 was that Christ, as the High Priest, was able to open a means for us to access God, tearing through the veil that separated us from the Holy of Holies, metaphorically speaking. In the following verses, you will find St. Paul giving us an additional reason for why Christ's priesthood was superior to that of the Old Testament.

10:11 And every priest stands ministering daily and offering repeatedly the same sacrifices, which can never take away sins. This verse is similar to verse one, but with one difference. The first verse of this chapter focused on the sacrifices that were offered continually year after year, which were nonetheless incapable of making those who approach perfect. Verse 11 here again reiterates the same concept about the ineffectiveness of the Levitical system, but instead of focusing on the inadequacy of the old covenant sacrifices, attention is drawn directly at the priests themselves and their own futility.

10:12 But this Man. This refers to Jesus Christ.

after He had offered one sacrifice for sins forever. Christ did not offer Himself on the cross repeatedly as a sacrifice to atone for our sins, but His sacrifice was sufficient to be offered once and be effective forever. That is why a person must refrain from speaking of the Divine Liturgy as involving an offering of a new sacrifice on the altar; it is recalling and reliving the same sacrifice of Christ that had already been offered *"once for all"* (Rom. 6:20; Heb. 7:27, 9:12, 10:10).

sat down at the right hand of God. Compare this verse with the previous one: there, the priests are said to be standing ministering and offering repeated sacrifices, whereas Christ took a seat after He offered His sacrifice. The fact that the priests are standing means that their job has not yet been completed. But when it is said about Christ that He *"sat down,"* it means His work has been accomplished and finished (which is what He said on the cross just before *"He gave up His spirit,"* saying, *"It is finished!"*—John 19:30). And this is the new point that added to the notion of the superiority of Christ's priesthood: Not only does the sacrifice of Christ suffice for all, but as a result of His sacrificial death, Jesus has taken His seat at the right hand of God. St. Paul refers here implicitly to the Psalm 110:1, which involves God the Father speaking to the hypostasis of Christ the Son: *"The LORD said to my Lord, "Sit at My right hand, till I make Your enemies Your footstool."* Having finished His work, exhibited by His having taken a seat, He is now sitting in the most dignified place of honor, signified by the *"right hand of God,"* being glorified in accordance with what Christ said in His famous prayer recorded in John 17: *"And now, O Father, glorify Me together with Yourself, with the glory which I had with You before the world was"* (John 17:5).

10:13 from that time waiting till His enemies are made His footstool. This refers to the latter portion of Psalm 110:1, where God the Father tells Christ to sit at His right hand until He subdues His enemies. Let me make a very important point, however. Christ, having said *"It is finished"* (John 19:3) as His last words on the cross and then taking His seat a the right hand of God, does not mean that all His enemies have already been finally subdued. St. Paul said that Christ *"must reign till He has put all enemies under His feet"* (1 Cor. 15:25), and *"the last enemy that will be destroyed is death"* (1 Cor. 15:26). This will be accomplished at the time that all of us will be raised again, so that death will cease to have any power over anyone anymore. Hence, not all enemies have already submitted to Christ, but when He said, *"It is finished"* (John 19:30), it referred to salvation being accomplished, and it was also the first step in achieving the promise that *"His enemies are made His footstool,"* because the enemy—death—is still, until now, the natural order of human existence. After all of His enemies have been subdued, He will then deliver the kingdom to God the Father, as St. Paul tells us in 1 Corinthians 15:24-26: *"Then comes the end, when He delivers the kingdom to God the Father, when He puts an end to all rule and all authority and power. For He must reign till He has put all enemies under His feet. The last enemy that will be destroyed is death."* Since the salvation accomplished on the cross has already been completed, we are confident that what is still to come—the submission of all enemies, including death—will also be fulfilled.

10:14 For by one offering He has perfected forever those who are being sanctified. By the offering of Christ's body, He has perfected us through sanctification. The Greek words for *"perfected"* and *"sanctified"* indicate a sense that this process of perfection and sanctification are an ongoing process. Because of His sacrifice, every time we sin, we can approach Him and receive forgiveness and become sanctified, and thus, Christ's salvation is one which we continually benefit from in our daily lives. Because of this, access to God, who is holy, is always available to us who likewise become holy through perfection and sanctification. Recall how in the Divine Liturgy according to St. Basil the Great as utilized in the Coptic Church, the priest says, *"the*

Holy for the Holies." This means that the body and blood of Christ (*"the Holies"*) can be taken by those who are made *"Holy"* through the continual process of perfection and sanctification. The Levitical system was incapable of perfecting us so that we could approach God, so that only the high priest, once a year, was allowed to enter into the Holy of Holies. We now, through the priesthood of Christ, are able to be perfected and sanctified so that we can have access to God.

10:15-18 St. Paul will refer again, in this set of verses, to the new covenant and its effectiveness in cleansing our conscience as it is compared with the old covenant.

10:15 But the Holy Spirit also witnesses to us. The words *"to us"* are very important because the Holy Spirit is here being described as speaking to each of us personally. As explained previously (see commentary on Heb. 3:7-11 discussing the word *"says,"* and also Heb. 9:8, *"the Holy Spirit indicating this"*), when you read the Bible, the Holy Spirit did not simply inspire the authors and that is all. No, but until now, every time you open the Bible and read it, the Holy Spirit speaks to you and bears witness to you through those words. Remember that the Holy Spirit is God, so if He bears witness, then whatever He says is absolutely true. This verse specifically can be understood to say that the Holy Spirit did not simply inspire Jeremiah (who is quoted in the following verses) to write about the new covenant, but until now, He bears witness to each of us about the new covenant.

for after He had said before. Notice how St. Paul refers to the Holy Spirit (indicated by the word *"He"*) as being the one who *"said"* the following Old Testament verses *"before,"* instead of saying that Jeremiah—the author attributed to writing these verses—said this before. That is because every word of Scripture can be considered the words of the Holy Spirit Himself, as St. Paul says to his disciple Timothy: *"All Scripture is given by inspiration of God"* (2 Tim. 3:16).

10:16-17 **"This is the covenant that I will make with them after those days, says the LORD: I will put My laws into their hearts, and in their minds I will write them," then He adds, "Their sins and their lawless deeds I will remember no more."** These verses are quoted from the prophecy found in the book of Jeremiah, 31:31-34. After God spoke about the new covenant to Jeremiah and said that He will write His laws into their hearts and minds, He said that their sins and iniquities will not be remembered anymore.

How do these words bear witness to the sacrifice of Christ? If you recall in Hebrews 10:3 that the sacrifices of the old covenant caused there to be a *"reminder of sins every year,"* which is a reminder for us and to God every time sin offerings were made to Him. Every time such offerings were made, it was a reminder of sins and not a true cleansing of them, and each time the aroma of such sacrifices reached God, they were also simply a reminder rather than having the effect of truly cleansing and remitting all the people's sins. But now, in the new covenant, *"their sins and their lawless deeds"* God *"will remember no more,"* because of the one-time offering of Christ's body presented to God on the cross. The Holy Spirit bore witness through the words of Jeremiah in the perfecting and sanctifying result of the sacrifice of Christ, so that in the new covenant, there is no remembrance of sins because the blood of Christ has the power to forgive all sins, for all people, for all ages (which is the meaning of Christ dying *"once for all"*—Rom. 6:20; Heb. 7:27, 9:12, 10:10). This perfection and sanctification, however, is an ongoing process in which we engage (see Heb. 10:14). The Holy Spirit who inspired Jeremiah, bears witness to each of us, and also brings this prophecy to reality.

10:18 **Now where there is remission of these, there is no longer an offering for sin.** Because our sins are forgiven, there is no need for an offering of sin. That is why there is no new offerings now for sin. As explained previously (see Heb. 10:12), the body and blood of Christ which is presented on the altar in every Divine Liturgy is not a new offering. At the end of the Divine Liturgy, the priest confesses his belief that the Eucharist is the same body offered once previously by Christ on the cross: "Amen. Amen. Amen. I believe, I believe, I believe, and confess to the last breath that this is the life-giving Flesh that Your only-begotten Son, our Lord, God and Savior Jesus Christ, took from our Lady, the Lady of us all, the holy Theotokos, Saint Mary." This is the same offering we relive and recall in every Divine Liturgy. God already shed His blood which is sufficient to forgive the sins of everyone forever. Hence, since Christ's one sacrifice accomplished the remission of sins, there is no longer a need to make any offerings for sin.

10:19-25 Verse 18 marked the end of St. Paul's theological discussion about the superiority of Christ's priesthood and sacrifice, and also the superiority of the new covenant over the old one. Let us recall what St. Paul has been focusing on thus far. St. Paul was addressing in this letter Jews who had become Christian. The letter was being sent to them with the overarching purpose of warning them not to apostatize—that is, not to return back to Judaism and forsake Christ. In all these chapters He utilized a number of arguments to persuade them about the superiority of Christianity over Judaism: the superiority of Christ over angels, Moses, Aaron, Joshua, etc., and also the superiority of His sacrifice and priesthood over those carried out during the time of the old covenant. Beginning now with verse 19, St Paul will draw some conclusions based on all his theological arguments. This method of focusing on theology first and then providing practical application afterward was common for St. Paul. We can learn from him a very important point regarding the study of theology. If you only study theology as a science in and of itself without applying that theology to your life, it is of no value. Rather, the purpose of studying doctrines and dogmas is to understand how they affect our personal lives. St. Paul will begin now to use the theological truth which he previously expounded on as the basis for his spiritual exhortation in the rest of the letter. This transition is implied in the word *"therefore,"* which begins verse 19.

10:19-21 **Therefore.** After understanding all of St. Paul's previous theological arguments and discussion, St. Paul begins now to provide a practical application of all he taught previously. After convincing them that the new covenant, Christ's priesthood, and His sacrifice are all superior to the old manner of doing things, *"therefore"* St. Paul has something to now tell the Hebrews, who were formerly Jews but had at that point already converted to Christianity.

brethren. This is a word that expresses love and closeness, which is meant to gain their attention. Also, he is recalling for them his previous mention of the notion that all Christians are brethren in Christ (for more, see commentary on Heb. 2:11, 2:12-13, 2:17) because in Him, we can call God our Father, while at the same time we call Christ our God, Lord, Master, and Savior.

having boldness to enter the Holiest ... and having a High Priest over the house of God. Here St. Paul is appealing to two important truths. First, we have a great *"High Priest over the house of God"* (v. 21). And what is the "house of God"? If you recall Hebrews 3:6, you would understand that God's house is us. Thus, if Christ is the great High Priest over His house, then He is our High Priest. The second truth St. Paul emphasizes is that we now have *"boldness to enter the Holiest."* St. Paul gives a few reasons why this is the case, as explained below.

by the blood of Jesus. (1) of 2. The first reason he gives is that we can enter the *"Holiest by the blood of Jesus."* In the Old Testament, the high priest could only enter into the Holy of Holies by shedding the blood of animals. But Jesus did not enter into the Holiest by the blood of animals, but by His own blood, thereby giving us open access to God and also boldness to approach God.

by a new and living way which He consecrated for us. (2) of 2. This is the second reason why we have *"boldness to enter the Holiest."* Christ opened for us a *"new and living way which He consecrated for us."* Christ is the pioneer and also at the same time the provider of this way: He was the first to enter the Holiest with boldness and is also the one who provides us a means to follow in His path as well. He leads all of us through this new way and means of access to God, as we say in the Divine Liturgy: *"Lead us throughout the way into Your kingdom."* Recall, of course, that Christ taught us, *"I am the way"* (John 14:6).

new. Christ has given us the opportunity to have something that was previously not available, which is direct access to God. Thus, this is a new means of accessing Him.

living. The path forged for us by Christ's sacrifice is *"living,"* because by following the living Christ (*"I am the ... life"*—John 14:6) in this *"new ... way"* we will also be granted life and salvation.

way. This means access to God. *"I am the way.... No one comes to the Father except through Me"* (John 14:6). So Christ is the *"way"* to the Father. Also note that during the earliest period of the Church, all the followers of Christ were called the followers of the *"Way,"* as you read in Acts 9:2.

through the veil. It is easy to understand this phrase, that Christ provided for us a new way *"through the veil."* In the Old Testament, there was a literal veil separating God from us, and Christ tore apart this veil literally and metaphorically when He sacrificed Himself on the cross (*"Then, behold, the veil of the temple was torn in two from top to bottom"*—Matt. 27:52; Mark 15:38).

that is, His flesh. There are two ways to understand this. Either it refers to the way, or it refers to the veil. Is St. Paul saying that His flesh is the way, or that His flesh is the veil? Actually, both are correct, but most of the Church Fathers preferred the second interpretation more, saying that His flesh refers to the veil. Before delving into that preferred interpretation, let us first examine the first manner by which we can understand this verse, which is that Christ's flesh is the way. Through Christ's flesh, now we have access to God. God prepared a body for the Son (see Heb. 10:5), and the Son offered this body for our sanctification. Now, this body became the *"way"* to heaven: *"Most assuredly, I say to you, unless you eat the flesh of the Son of Man and drink His blood, you have no life in you"* (John 6:53). But what does it mean to say that word *"flesh"* here refers to the veil? The flesh of Christ can be considered as referencing our humanity, which He shared. This humanity, because of all its weakness, could not carry out God's will. But Christ took our humanity, perfected it, sanctified it, and on the cross pierced it in order to open a way to God through His flesh (as if our humanity was a veil that was previously hindering us), in order to regain access to God. This flesh that was pierced gushed forth water and blood for our sanctification, granting us Baptism (water) and Communion (blood); and note that St. Paul will speak about how we were *"sprinkled from an evil conscience"* in v. 22 below. This veil was pierced on the cross, died, and rose again on the third day to open the way. The veil that was separating us from God, which is the weakness of our humanity, was taken and pierced in order to open a way for us in order to allow us a manner to approach God the Father. ✣ Notice the three times that St. Paul mentioned the body of Christ and how he develops the deeper concept and significance of the body of Christ: first (in Heb. 10:5), when Christ entered into the world (through His incarnation), the Father prepared a body for the Son; then, this body was offered by Christ (as explained in Heb. 10:14) on the cross for our perfection and sanctification; and now (as explained here in this verse) through this body, we have a *"new and living way."* That is why we have the body of Christ with us every day on the altar; because it is our only access to God. There is no other means of access to God except through His body, which is why He left His body for us on the altar to partake of every day.

10:22-25 St. Paul, having laid out the foundation of his spiritual exhortation to the Hebrews by explaining that we have a High Priest by whom we can enter the Holiest with boldness through a *"new and living way,"* which is His flesh, now there are three things St. Paul says we should do. First, we should *"draw near to God"* (v.22). Now that we have access to God, *"let us draw near"* to Him. You can approach God! You can abide in Him and He in you! Now you have boldness and access and a new and living way! Now you have a High Priest at the right hand of the Father who intercedes with His blood at all times! So then *"let us draw near"* to God. Doing so, we are enabled to do two other important things. We can hold fast the confession of our faith (from v. 23, telling these Christians who came from Judaism that they should not return back to Judaism and deny the Lord Christ). And also, with this newfound courage, we should encourage one another (v. 24) to maintain and hold fast the faith. The pressure of persecution was severe at that time and many people considered returning to Judaism; but now, knowing they have boldness to enter the Holiest, and knowing that they now have the great and superior High Priest who is above all others, they should encourage one another to refrain from apostasy.

10:22 let us draw near. Now the door is open and the veil is torn apart. Can't we simply just enter? Recall the parable the Lord gave about the king who arranged a marriage for his son: *"But when the king came in to see the guests, he saw a man there who did not have on a wedding garment. So he said to him, 'Friend, how did you come in here without a wedding garment?' And he was speechless. Then the king said to the servants, 'Bind him hand and foot, take him away, and cast him into outer darkness; there will be weeping and gnashing of teeth.' For many are called, but few are chosen"* (Matt. 22:11-14). Drawing near to God requires certain measures that we need to take. St. Paul is trying to motivate people who are already Christian to draw near to God, indicating that simply being a Christian is not sufficient for us to gain the benefits of the new covenant and Christ's sacrifice. What follows is an explanation of the *"steps of the faith"* that people must take (Rom. 4:12).

with a true heart in full assurance of faith. (1) of 3. This refers to genuine faith that lacks any doubt (with "assurance").

having our hearts sprinkled from an evil conscience. (2) of 3. We should have our inner man cleansed, which we know to be effectuated through the Mysteries of Repentance and Confession, and the Eucharist.

and our bodies washed with pure water. (3) of 3. This implies the Mystery of Baptism. Although St. Paul in a sense speaks of the inner part of man as needing cleansing, then speaks of the outer body needing washing (through Baptism), this in no way means that Baptism only involves outer cleansing, but it is the *"the washing of regeneration and renewing of the Holy Spirit"* of one's inner self first and foremost (Titus 3:5).

10:23 Let us hold fast the confession. Not only does drawing near to God enable us to hold firmly the confession of our faith, but there is a reciprocal relationship here whereby holding fast to our faith, we will be drawn nearer to God. As drawing close to God will make me strong enough to hold fast to my faith, also when I hold fast to my faith, I will find myself getting closer to God.

of our hope. Our hope is eternal life with God. Let us then hold fast to Christ, hoping and believing that through Him we will receive eternal life.

without wavering, for He who promised is faithful. This emphasizes the theme of this epistle whereby St. Paul is trying to keep the formerly

Jewish Christians from returning back to Judaism. Thus, he implores that they hold fast to their Christian beliefs and trust in Christ *"without wavering."* We do this knowing that He who promised us eternal life is reliable and dependable.

10:24 And let us consider one another. In this way, we will be saved together. We are all members in the body of Christ. This membership and fellowship of the believers is very important for our salvation. The great St. Paul himself appealed to the Romans for mutual encouragement: *"that I may be encouraged together with you by the mutual faith both of you and me"* (Rom. 1:12). Supporting each other will allow us to *"grow"* together *"in all things into Him who is the head—Christ"* (Eph. 4:15).

in order to stir up love and good works. The reason St. Paul exhorts us to encourage one another mutually is *"in order to stir up love and good works."*

❖ *The atmosphere in the church* ~ Here, I would like to mention an important point regarding the atmosphere in the church. If you enter a church and you find an atmosphere of hypocrisy, judgment, and gossip, such an atmosphere fails to stir up love and good works in people. People contributing to such an atmosphere cannot be considered to be true disciples and children of Christ: *"By this all will know that you are My disciples, if you have love for one another"* (John 13:35). We, as believers, need to ensure that we create an atmosphere of love and good works. It is not enough to know true dogmas and doctrines, but if these true dogmas and doctrines are not translated into practical application, it will be unprofitable, and thus, of no avail.

10:25 not forsaking the assembling of ourselves together, as is the manner of some. Usually, when the Bible references an assembly of believers, it indicates the Divine Liturgy. In the Divine Liturgy, we all assemble together literally and also spiritually, becoming unified in the Communion. Thus, we can read this verse as saying, "If some people do not show up for the Liturgy, it is your responsibility to stir them up and encourage them to attend." This is not only the priest's responsibility, but all of us should encourage each other for the betterment of our spiritual lives.

but exhorting one another, and so much the more as you see the Day approaching. St. Paul speaks of the Second Coming of Christ, saying that we need to exhort one another and eagerly encourage one another to grow in good works.

❖ *Our responsibility to each other in the church*~ This and the immediately preceding verses are very important in delineating our responsibilities as congregants in the church. We are each responsible for every person in the body of Christ. Do not repeat what Cain said, *"Am I my brother's keeper?"* (Gen. 4:9). Yes, we each have a responsibility to our brothers and sisters in the church, encouraging them to attend the meetings and liturgies in the church.

10:26-31 St. Paul will now return to his main theme and give a fourth warning (out of a total of five—see commentary on Heb. 2:1) against apostasy. The first warning was the danger of neglect (Heb. 2:1-4); the second was the danger of unbelief (Heb. 3:7-19); and the third was the danger of not maturing (Heb. 5:11-14). Now, in this next set of verses, St. Paul will discuss the danger of shrinking back.

10:26 **For if we sin.** The word *"sin"* here does not refers to someone who suffers a momentary slip contrary to God's commandments, but rather indicates a persistent and continual pattern of sinfulness. The main sin which St. Paul refers to here is apostasy, as will be explained in the verses that follow.

willfully. St. Paul is speaking of willful sins, reflecting on Numbers 15:27-31 (for more, see commentary on Heb. 9:6-7: *"committed in ignorance"*).

after we have received the knowledge of the truth, there no longer remains a sacrifice for sins. If we abide in the continual and willful denial of Christ after we have received the knowledge of the truth regarding the superiority of the new covenant and Christ over the old covenant, and that only through Christ can we reach the Father, then *"there no longer remains a sacrifice for sins."* If a person rejects Christ as the means of salvation, then there no longer remains any hope in salvation for him as there is no other way made available. (St. Paul is not saying that a person who apostatizes will not be accepted if he returns to Christ and He accepts him again, but he discussed earlier in this epistle about the practical impossibility of such a return to Christ ever happening. For more, see commentary on Hebrews 6:4-8).

10:27 **but a certain fearful expectation of judgment, and fiery indignation which will devour the adversaries.** If a person rejects Christ willfully and maintains this rejection, he is bringing upon himself condemnation and judgment. Unlike a believer, who is eagerly waiting of the Second Coming of the Lord Christ (as St. Paul discusses at the end of this chapter), St. Paul is saying that a person who rejects Christ can only expect punishment along with a *"fearful expectation of judgment."* Those who resist the Holy Spirit and deny Christ, abiding in sin, rightly fear *"fiery indignation."*

10:28 Anyone who has rejected Moses' law dies without mercy on the testimony of two or three witnesses. Here St. Paul is referring to Deuteronomy 17:2-6, which in summary says that anyone who rejects Moses's law will die without mercy. The full text is provided as follows: *"If there is found among you, within any of your gates which the LORD your God gives you, a man or a woman who has been wicked in the sight of the LORD your God, in transgressing His covenant, who has gone and served other gods and worshiped them, either the sun or moon or any of the host of heaven, which I have not commanded, and it is told you, and you hear of it, then you shall inquire diligently. And if it is indeed true and certain that such an abomination has been committed in Israel, then you shall bring out to your gates that man or woman who has committed that wicked thing, and shall stone to death that man or woman with stones. Whoever is deserving of death shall be put to death on the testimony of two or three witnesses; he shall not be put to death on the testimony of one witness."*

10:29 Of how much worse punishment, do you suppose, will he be thought worthy. Moses's law, which is less (in every respect) than the way made accessible by Christ's sacrifice. Then, if the punishment for rejecting the former is so great, how much worse will the punishment be for the person rejecting the greater—Christ.

who has trampled the Son of God underfoot, counted the blood of the covenant by which he was sanctified a common thing, and insulted the Spirit of grace? Notice how St. Paul describes apostasy. It is quite frightful actually. He says apostasy is trampling the Son of God underfoot: the Son of God who came to the world to save me, if I do not believe in Him, it is as if I am trampling on Him. Not only that, by rejecting Christ, such a person is considered to be deeming the precious blood of Christ which He shed on behalf of all of us as a common thing. Finally, St. Paul describes apostasy as insulting the Holy Spirit, because it is He who takes the advantages of Christ's salvation and gives it to us (through the Mysteries).

10:30 For we know Him who said, "Vengeance is Mine, I will repay," says the Lord. And again, "The LORD will judge His people." These words are derived from Deuteronomy 32:35-36. St. Paul is addressing the Hebrews, who again as explained previously were Jewish converts to Christianity, as people who "know Him," for they were familiar with the Old Testament and its writings. Rejecting Christ and falling into apostasy will lead a person to be judged severely. For truly God *"has appointed a Day for recompense on which He will appear to judge the world in righteousness, and give each one according to his deeds"* (as the priest prays in the Divine Liturgy).

10:31 It is a fearful thing to fall into the hands of the living God. It is fearful to the sinners and to those who reject Christ to fall into the hands of the living God. But for believers, it is by no means fearful.

10:32-39 In order to persuade the recipients of his epistle to refrain from falling into the sin of apostasy, he at times gives them harsh warnings, and yet at other times he encourages them, appealing to them by mentioning their positive attributes. After warning them about the danger of shrinking back, he appeals to their previous exhibition of the virtue of perseverance.

10:32 But recall the former days in which, after you were illuminated, you endured a great struggle with sufferings. *"Illuminated"* here refers to Baptism, as it is referred to as the Mystery of Illumination. Hence, we can replaced the word "illuminated" here with the word Baptism, so that we read the verse as saying, "But recall the former days in which, after you were baptized, you endured a great struggle with sufferings." Usually when we start with Christ, we begin with great fervor, but then gradually develop a lukewarm attitude in our Christian endeavors. St. Paul is appealing to their previous perseverance so that they should continue to be faithful and not let the present persecution accomplish what the previous one had failed to do, which is to tempt them to return to Judaism.

10:33 partly while you were made a spectacle both by reproaches and tribulations, and partly while you became companions of those who were so treated. St. Paul is telling them to remember their former faithfulness to Christ and not be jaded by the current pressure to return back to Judaism. After they were baptized, they were able to endure through the grace of God. He reminds them of their perseverance and what they endured. Whether they faced persecution directly (being made a *"spectacle by reproaches and tribulations"*), or whether they supported those who were suffering persecution (having become *"companions of those who were so treated"*), that was regarded by God as a great measure of perseverance and struggle for His name.

10:34 for you had compassion on me in my chains. St. Paul is trying to persuade the Hebrews to endure persecution and not return to Judaism, reminding them of how they supported him during his own persecution. When we support a person who is persecuted for Christ, it is considered suffering for Christ even if we ourselves are not facing direct persecution.

and joyfully accepted the plundering of your goods. The Hebrews did not accept to support St. Paul during his times of persecution simply out of a sense of obligation, but they did so joyfully. Many times, people accept suffering only because they have no other option, but here, St. Paul is not speaking of passive acceptance of suffering, but the active and joyful acceptance of suffering.

knowing that you have a better and an enduring possession for yourselves in heaven. St. Paul reminds the Hebrews for the reason they previously were motivated to endure suffering and why they should continue to strive in their endurance. We need to shift our focus to heaven, and when we do so, we will accept our suffering joyfully. That is what happened with St. Stephen when he looked at heaven and saw the glory that is prepared for the saints, and therefore, willingly accepted the suffering with joy, asking God not to count it as a sin against his persecutors, knowing that by their actions he was gaining so much benefit: *"When they heard these things they were cut to the heart, and they gnashed at him with their teeth. But he, being full of the Holy Spirit, gazed into heaven and saw the glory of God, and Jesus standing at the right hand of God, and said, "Look! I see the heavens opened and the Son of Man standing at the right hand of God!"* (Acts 7:54-56). (Note that St. Stephen's death was consented to by Saul, who later became the great St. Paul, writing these words in this epistle—Acts 8:1). St. Paul is telling us that our hope in heaven and our continual focus on our eternal inheritance is what will allow us to remain steadfast during our times of persecution.

10:35 Therefore do not cast away your confidence, which has great reward. The confidence in our eternal inheritance, knowing that we have *"boldness to enter the Holiest by the blood of Jesus,"* we must not cast away our confidence. Holding fast to such confidence will allow us to reap *"great reward,"* which is the indescribable eternal bliss awaiting us after our lives here on earth.

10:36 For you have need of endurance. You need endurance. The mentality of the people when the church suffers, speaking particularly about the Copts in Egypt, is, *"How can we get rid of this suffering? How can we end it?"* St. Paul gives the Hebrews a completely different approach. He does not tell them means to resist the suffering and how to effectuate its end, but rather how to endure and accept the suffering joyfully. He implores them to endure suffering, not to resist it.

so that after you have done the will of God, you may receive the promise. This can be regarded as a reference to what he spoke about earlier in this chapter about how Christ accepted the will of God (in Heb. 10:9): *"Behold, I have come to do Your will, O God."* That will of the Father was in preparing a body for Christ from Him to offer as a sacrifice. "You asked Me to die, and I accepted to die, because that is Your will." That was His prayer in Gethsemane: *"not My will, but Yours, be done"* (Luke 22:42). As Christ fulfilled the will of God, this is also the will of God that St. Paul says applies for the Hebrews to whom he is writing. That will of God is that they suffer for His name, to carry their cross, as Christ said, *"If anyone desires to come after Me, let him deny himself, and take up his cross daily, and follow Me"* (Luke 9:23). St. Paul implores them to accept the will of God as Christ did. If they do so, they will receive honor in heaven as Christ also received honor in heaven after he had *"done the will of God."*

10:37 "For yet a little while, and He who is coming will come and will not tarry. These verses come from Habakkuk 2:3-4, according to the Septuagint version of the Old Testament available at the time. St. Paul appeals to the Second Coming of Christ. For the faithful, it is a joyful day and a day of deliverance. He tells them to endure, waiting because only *"a little while"* from now *"He who is coming will come."* He tries to motivate them to remember that our suffering is temporary, but Christ will come again and all suffering will cease for those who love Him, and our bliss will then be eternal.

10:38 Now the just shall live by faith. If you are righteous, you need to live by the faith in the Second Coming of Christ. *"Amen ... come, Lord Jesus!"* (Rev. 22:20). That faith should speak to our hearts as follows: "I know that You are coming to deliver me from the suffering that is in the world. I know that You are coming, in order to reward me for all these days of tribulation that I am enduring. I am awaiting your coming. I am living with this faith."

But if anyone draws back, My

soul has no pleasure in him. This is another iteration of the theme of St. Paul's epistle, which is an attempt to persuade these new converts to Christianity not to return to their former religion (i.e., Judaism, from which they converted). For those who return back to Judaism, or return to their former lives of denying Christ and do so for the remainder of their time on earth, God says, *"My soul has no pleasure in him."*

10:39 But we are not of those who draw back to perdition, but of those who believe to the saving of the soul. We are not apostates, but we are among the believers who have faith, which will deliver us from perdition. Here St. Paul sets the stage for the saving faith about which He will speak in the next chapter.

✤ *Are you joyful or fearful of Christ's Second Coming?* ~ Is the thought of the Day of the Second Coming of Christ a fearful one or a joyful one for you? If Christ comes this moment, right now, will you be among the fearful, afraid of His Second coming, or among the joyful, who will rejoice in His Second Coming? For those who abide in sin, this Day is a fearful day; for those who abide in the faith of Christ, this Day will be received with joy and happiness.

Chapter 10 Questions

1. Why can't the blood of bulls and goats actually take away sin?

2. What was the function of the veil in Old Testament worship?

3. What is the significance of the veil being ripped in two at the time of Jesus' crucifixion?

4. Why is our access to God called a "new and living way"?

5. Why is perseverance so important?

11

Chapter Outline

- Definition of faith (1-3)
- Faith before the flood (4-7)
- The faith of the patriarchs (8-22)
- The faith of Moses (23-29)
- Other examples of faith (30-38)
- The promise is Christ (39-40)

Introduction

St. Paul concluded Chapter 10 by saying that *"the just shall live by faith"* (v. 38), and also that faith is important in saving our souls. Now in Chapter 11, St. Paul will elaborate more on faith and how it works in the lives of the believers. St. Paul will pay special attention to the relationship between faith and endurance, as well as faith and perseverance, because he is writing to Christians from a Jewish origin who are facing persecution and pressure to return back to Judaism. Those who are considering apostasy to escape the pains of persecution need such a message regarding faith.

11:1 Now faith is the substance of things hoped for, the evidence of things not seen. This can be considered a definition of the term *"faith."* We are confident and sure that what we are hoping for, we will receive. This confidence is not only objective, but it is also subjective. In other words, when we believe in the eternal kingdom, the objective reality is that yes, we believe that there is such a thing as an eternal kingdom; but the subjective confidence is that we believe God's promises that if we follow Him, we will inherit the eternal kingdom. Faith is, then, the confident assurance of the promises for which we are hoping. It is an inner conviction about the things that cannot be seen. Most of us have not seen Christ, or the angels, or the eternal life, or the Paradise of Joy, but from within, we are confident that these things exist. This is because He who promised is reliable and faithful. Faith is, thus, a life that does not wait for human evidence or proof. I am not waiting for evidence in the lab in order to believe. Rather, faith accepts the word of God as totally sufficient evidence. It is enough that God said so, and because He said so, I believe.

11:2 For by it the elders obtained a good testimony. God approved and supported the elders of the past whose lives exhibited the faith in the things not seen as described in the previous verse. When Abraham *"believed in the Lord,"* God *"accounted it to him for righteousness"* (Gen. 15:6; see also Rom. 4:1 and Gal. 3:6). This means that God approved the faith of Abraham. So, when we believe, then God will bear testimony or witness of us that we are also righteous. In this way, when we believe, we are considered to be pleasing God.

11:2 By faith we understand that the worlds were framed by the word of God, so that the things which are seen were not made of things which are visible. The world that we see right now was created out of nothing. There was no pre-existing material which God utilized to form the world. The things *"which are seen,"* that is, the creation of God which we see before us, were not created out of visible material, but rather out of nothing. From the unseen, God put into existence what we see right now. Hence, if God was able to create from nothing what we see right now, then when we believe in the yet unseen, we can be confident that God will bring it to reality in the fullness of time. The things in which faith believes (i.e., the unseen things under God's hand created by His word) will one day be seen. For the world, seeing is believing; but for us, believing is confidence in knowing what God has told us, so that even when we cannot see those promises, we believe simply because the one who promised such things is reliable (Heb. 10:23). This was the mentality of Thomas, who said, *"Unless I see in His hands the print of the nails, and put my finger into the print of the nails, and put my hand into His side, I will not believe"* (John 20:25).

11:4-38 After the introduction about faith provided in the previous three verses, St. Paul begins to give examples regarding the heroes of faith. We can classify these examples as follows: faith before the flood; the faith of the patriarchs; the faith of Moses; and then other examples exhibiting faith.

11:4 By faith Abel offered to God a more excellent sacrifice than Cain, through which he obtained witness that he was righteous, God testifying of his gifts. Abel offered a bloody sacrifice of an animal, but Cain did not do so; rather, he offered from the *"fruit of the ground"* (Gen. 4:3). After the sin of Adam and Eve, we read in the book of Genesis that, *"God made tunics of skin, and clothed them"* (Gen. 3:21). Where did God get this skin to clothe Adam and Eve with? Obviously, it had to come from an animal. Holy tradition teaches us that, in this way, God taught Adam and Eve that without the shedding of blood, there is no forgiveness. He also taught them how to offer a sacrifice. After teaching them how to offer a burnt offering, He took the skin from it and made clothes for Adam and Eve. They then taught their children, including Abel and Cain, to offer animal sacrifices. Abel, by faith, believed in the coming of the Messiah, because God promised Adam and Eve that the offspring of the woman will bruise the head of the serpent (Gen. 3:15). Thus, Abel, by faith, believed in the coming of the Messiah, and through the shedding of blood, there is forgiveness. That is why Abel offered a bloody sacrifice. Cain, however, did not. That is why Abel is said to have offered *"a more excellent sacrifice than Cain."* By doing this, *"he obtained witness"* before God that *"he was righteous"* (as explained in v. 2, meaning that God indicated His approval of Abel). He was righteous because of his faith which was demonstrated in his obedience to the word of God.

and through it he being dead still speaks. St. Paul is referring here to what God said to Cain, *"What have you done? The voice of your brother's blood cries out to Me from the ground"* (Gen. 4:10). Even after Abel was killed, his blood cried out to God. Actually, in Chapter 12, St. Paul will speak about the blood of Abel that speaks (Heb. 12:24). When we trust the Lord, even physical death will not stop us from speaking and bearing witness to God, as the blood of the martyrs bear witness until today to the faith, and as the blood of Abel bears witness to his faith and righteousness.

11:5 By faith Enoch was taken away so that he did not see death, "and was not found, because God had taken him"; for before he was taken he had this testimony, that he pleased God. Maybe because St. Paul mentioned Abel who was killed, he afterward mentions Enoch who has yet to die, but was taken up to heaven alive. What is written about Enoch is so little. We read in the book of Genesis that Enoch *"walked with God; and he was not, for God took him"* (Gen. 5:24). *"Walked with God"* means that he trusted God and had confidence in Him, which is why he followed Him; when you trust in someone, only then will you follow him. So, Enoch trusted God, and this trust is faith. That is why God took him alive to heaven, because he pleased God. As I mentioned previously, simply believing in God is pleasing to Him.

11:6 But without faith it is impossible to please Him. If you do not trust God, how can you please Him? Faith is to be confident in Him, but if you do not trust God, how can you please Him? St. Paul then says two things about our faith in God.

for he who comes to God must believe that He is. (1) of 2. In Chapter 10, St. Paul implores the Hebrews to *"draw near"* to God *"with a true heart in full assurance of faith"* (Heb. 10:22). Now he does not simply ask people to come to God, but adds another layer by telling people the attitude we should have when we approach Him. You come to God with faith, because it is impossible to please Him otherwise. We must believe that God exists and is the creator and founder of this entire world, visible and invisible. If you want to come to God, you need to believe first that He exists, that He is faithful, and that His promises are true; and even if you do not see it before your eyes now, you need to believe that it is true.

and that He is a rewarder of those who diligently seek Him. (2) of 2. St. Paul here is saying to the Hebrews, if they diligently seek God and endure persecution, they will be rewarded by God; and this trust in God's reward will motivate us to persevere. What motivates students to excel? It is the confidence that by their efforts, they will receive a rewarding outcome. In a similar way, our confidence in the kingdom of heaven and our eternal inheritance will help us endure and persevere all the difficult times of persecution.

11:7 By faith Noah, being divinely warned of things not yet seen, moved with godly fear, prepared an ark for the saving of his household. Again St. Paul uses the phrase *"not yet seen,"* reiterating his definition of faith (given in the first three verses). God warned Noah and the world around him that He would flood the world. Noah believed God, although he did not see the flood yet, and started to build the ark. The message here to the Hebrews is, "If you deny Christ and reject Him, then there will be judgment (as mentioned in Heb. 10:27), but if you believe in Christ, drawing close to Him and becoming steadfast in the faith, you will be rewarded." So, let us follow the example of Noah who believed in God about things not yet seen, being moved by godly fear, obeying the warning of God about the *"unseen"* (*"The fear of the LORD is the beginning of wisdom"*—Psalm 111:10). The fear of God means to respect Him, revering Him and trusting Him. The fear of God is related to faith in that such fear and also reverence to God propels one to believe Him.

by which he condemned the world. When you act on your faith, then you will be saved, just as Noah acted on his faith and built the ark, saving himself and his household. And that is the message St. Paul wants to give to the Hebrews. Only eight people were saved in the ark, but the world did not believe Him and were thus *"condemned."*

11:8-22 After this, St. Paul begins to speak about the faith of the patriarchs, after the flood, with a special focus on Abraham.

11:8 By faith Abraham obeyed when he was called to go out to the place which he would receive as an inheritance. And he went out, not knowing where he was going. If Abraham did not trust God, do you think he would have obeyed and followed Him even though he did not know where he was going? When God called Abraham, he did not tell him where exactly he would live. But it was enough that God called him, and so he agreed to follow Him regardless of where he would end up. Obedience here, which is the result of faith, is what St. Paul wanted to emphasize in this verse. If you have faith, you will obey. If you do not obey, you do not have faith. Faith is trusting God enough to obey Him. When a son or daughter trusts their father, they will obey him without questioning him. In the same way, if we trust God enough, we will obey Him similarly without question.

11:9 By faith he dwelt in the land of promise as in a foreign country, dwelling in tents with Isaac and Jacob, the heirs with him of the same promise. Abraham made choices in his life based only on the promise of God and not on the fulfillment of the promise. He left his country and chose to live as a stranger and foreigner in an unknown land, living in tents because of his faith in God. St. Paul is telling the Hebrews, "Now you have a promise, which is that you will inherit the kingdom of heaven, and this promise will not be fulfilled in your lifetime; so if you are going to wait until the fulfillment of the promise and then act on your faith, this is then not faith." Faith is to act on the promise before its fulfillment, as Abraham obeyed God before he saw the land.

11:10 for he waited for the city which has foundations, whose builder and maker is God. St. Paul now elevates our mind from thinking about the earthly promised land to the heavenly one. The earthly promised land is actually a symbol (or type) of heaven and eternal life. As Abraham lived as a stranger and foreigner, we hear live as strangers and foreigners, because we do not have a permanent dwelling here on earth, but rather are looking forward to the permanent city built by God, *"For our citizenship is in heaven, from which we also eagerly wait for the Savior, the Lord Jesus Christ"* (Phil. 3:20). Abraham, with the eye of faith, saw the earthly promised land as a type (i.e., example) of the eternal promised land—the heavenly one.

11:11 By faith Sarah herself also received strength to conceive seed, and she bore a child when she was past the age, because she judged Him faithful who had promised. Some people say this verse is not actually about Sarah but more so about Abraham, because Sarah laughed when God spoke to Abraham (Gen. 18:12). So, they read it in this way: "By the faith of Abraham, Sarah herself also received strength to conceive seed, etc." However, Sarah, in the beginning, although she laughed, she afterward believed, as St. Paul says here, *"she judged Him faithful who had promised."* St. Paul is showing us here how God is loving enough to embrace our moments of unbelief or weakness at which time we lack faith in God. Recall the story in Mark Chapter 9 of the father whose son was demon possessed; he brought his son to the Lord and the Lord told him, *"If you can believe, all things are possible to him who believes,"* and then, after quickly examining himself, *"Immediately the father of the child cried out and said with tears, 'Lord, I believe; help my unbelief!'"* (Mark 9:23-24). So, in reality, he was lacking belief, which is why he asked the Lord to help his unbelief. Sarah was also having trouble believing in the beginning how in her old age she could conceive, but after this, *"she judged Him faithful who had promised."* This faith gave her *"strength to conceive seed, and she bore a child when she was past the age."*

11:12 Therefore from one man, and him as good as dead, were born as many as the stars of the sky in multitude—innumerable as the sand which is by the seashore. Abraham, who with regard to procreation, was no more capable of producing offspring with Sarah than a dead man. Therefore, from Abraham and Sarah, who were considered as if their bodies were dead, unable to have children as many as any two other dead bodies, brought forth children as innumerable as the stars in the sky and the sand of the sea. Here, St. Paul is trying to say how faith is great, able to bring life out of death. So, even if you are persecuted to the point of death, God will bring you back to life.

11:13 These all died. Abel, Noah, Abraham, Sarah, Isaac, and Jacob (not Enoch, as he did not die).

in faith, not having received the promises, but having seen them afar off were assured of them, embraced them. St. Paul is especially rebuking our generation who are so used to instant gratification: if we want something, we need to have it now. However, true trust in God does not require Him to fulfill His promises here and now. For us strangers and pilgrims, the here and now is not what that which has been promised to us, but rather things which are "afar off" in the age to come. We trust in these promises because He who made them is reliable.

and confessed that they were strangers and pilgrims on the earth. We are *"strangers and pilgrims on the earth,"* because here, we do not have a permanent dwelling place. The fulfillment of the promises of God will be realized in the age to come.

11:14 For those who say such things. This pertains to those who say that they are *"strangers and pilgrims on the earth"* (Heb. 11:13).

declare plainly that they seek a homeland. If we are saying we are strangers and pilgrims or sojourners, we can then be said to implicitly be indicating a longing for a homeland, which is being sought out.

11:15-16 And truly if they had called to mind that country from which they had come out, they would have had opportunity to return. But now they desire a better, that is, a heavenly country. Those who called themselves strangers (see v. 13), if they considered the original city and country from which they came as being their homeland, they would have returned to it and no longer felt like a sojourner. But since they did not return to their original city from which God called Abraham, that means they *"desire a better, that is, a heavenly country."* Let me try to say it in other words: Abraham, Sarah, Isaac, Jacob, etc—these people—after leaving their country, confessed that they are strangers and pilgrims. Are they saying we are strangers and pilgrims because they left their birth country? If they called their birth country their homeland, they would have returned to it and no longer felt as if they were strangers and pilgrims. But they did not return to it. Then what was their home? Their true homeland was this city—the heavenly country—which was made by God. That is why in the Divine Liturgy we pray, *"Those, O Lord, whose souls You have taken, repose them in the paradise of joy, in the region of the living forever, in the heavenly Jerusalem—in that place,"* and then we follow that by praying, *"And we too, who are sojourners in this place, keep us in Your faith, and grant us Your peace unto the end."* We are sojourners here because our home is heaven.

Therefore God is not ashamed to be called their God. When we trust in God, even though we do not see the fulfillment of God's promises in front of our eyes, God will not be ashamed to be called our God. Here, St. Paul is reminding them of the covenant between Him and us. The terms of the covenant is that if we do our part, then we will be His people and He will be our God (see Heb. 8:10; see also Rev. 21:3, which says, *"Behold, the tabernacle of God is with men, and He will dwell with them, and they shall be His people. God Himself will be with them and be their God"*). If we do not believe in God and in His promises, then God will be ashamed to call Himself our God.

✥ *Is God ashamed to say He is our God?* ~ Ask yourself: do our choices make God ashamed to be called our God? Let us examine the choices we make everyday. God was not ashamed to be called the God of Abraham, Isaac, and Jacob. Usually a person relates himself to someone who is higher. For example, a person would say, "I am the son of the president," but important men rarely will be found to describe themselves in relation to someone inferior to them. But when God appeared to Moses, He said, *"I am the God of Abraham, the God of Isaac, and the God of Jacob"* (Ex. 3:6), as if God was happy and receiving glory in relating Himself to us. If He had said to Moses, "I am God," that would be more than enough! But God introduced Himself as the God of these patriarchs. St. Paul is saying here then that God is not ashamed to be called their God, being happy to say that He is the God of these great men. Would God be happy to claim you and say that He is your God? If I have faith in Him and obey Him, God will not be ashamed to identify and present Himself as my God.

for He has prepared a city for them. This city which has been prepared is heaven.

11:17 By faith Abraham, when he was tested, offered up Isaac, and he who had received the promises offered up his only begotten son. In Hebrews 11:8, St. Paul spoke of Abraham's faith. Here, he mentions his faith again, but focuses on a slightly different aspect. Before, when he spoke about the promised land, Abraham did not receive the fulfillment of the promise at all. But God promised Abraham with something else too: that He would give him a son. And Abraham actually received the fulfillment of this promise, in that his son Isaac was born to him. Here is the big difference between the previous mention of Abraham's faith and the mention of it here: God is asking Abraham to offer the fulfillment of His promise as a sacrifice, appearing to be withdrawing the fulfillment of the promise to Abraham from him. Is Abraham's faith going to be steadfast or shaken? This was his test of faith. The sacrifice of Isaac was a tremendous test for Abraham, as he was asked to offer the only promise of God that was fulfilled during his lifetime—the "here and now." God asked him to give Isaac up and trust in Him without seeing or possessing the fulfillment of the promise. What does St. Paul highlight here? For Abraham, God's promise is more important than its fulfillment. Trusting Him who promised should be more important than possessing the fulfillment of the promise. Many times for us, the fulfillment of the promise is more important than the giver of the promise (i.e., God). Not so with Abraham. When God asked to withdraw the promise again, Abraham obeyed, because he trusted in Him with regard to all things.

11:18-19 of whom it was said, "In Isaac your seed shall be called," concluding that God was able to raise him up, even from the dead. In spite of the promise of God that He would give Abraham a son through whom Abraham would become the father of many nations, he was not reluctant to offer him as a sacrifice. He trusted that God, who is not a liar and therefore, when He says, *"In Isaac your seed shall be called,"* the only conclusion is that if he died, God would raise him up again from the dead. Here, St. Paul is highlighting another important point about the faith of Abraham. When God asked him to offer up Isaac as a sacrifice, Abraham had two options: (1) to believe that God withdrew His promise; (2) to believe that God is committed to His promise so that even if Isaac died, He would raise him from the dead. But Abraham did not choose the first option because it would have been a failure in the test of faith. ❖ Do you trust God in the same way? Do you trust in Him that even if you are martyred for His name, that He will raise you up as Abraham trusted God?

from which he also received him in a figurative sense. Although Isaac did not die literally, it was as if he was dead figuratively, being committed to death as he laid bound on the wood on the altar ready to be delivered up as a burnt offering to God. From there, after God halted the sacrifice, Isaac was taken up again from the altar, received as if figuratively he had come back from the dead. Here, Isaac became a type and symbol of Christ, who was also was laid on a wood and offered Himself a sacrifice, after which time He was also received again by His resurrection from the dead.

11:20 By faith Isaac blessed Jacob and Esau concerning things to come. If you recall, Esau was the firstborn, while Jacob was born second. But by faith, Isaac gave him the blessing belonging to the firstborn. A person may retort, "But Jacob tricked his father to receive the blessing." However, even when Esau returned and was present in front of Isaac, Isaac, nonetheless, affirmed his blessing of Jacob. He had faith in knowing that the second Adam (or *"last Adam"*—1 Cor. 15:45) would descend from Jacob and *"become the firstfruits of those who have fallen asleep"* (1 Cor. 15:20). Esau then represents the first Adam, and Christ represents the second Adam. When Isaac blessed Jacob, the second son, it was as if Isaac was prophesying *"concerning things to come,"* regarding how Christ, the second Adam, would be our blessed firstfruit, much as Jacob, the second born son was given the firstborn blessing instead of the first son, Esau. In other words, the second son (Jacob) was blessed over the first son (Esau) as if he was the firstborn; likewise Christ (the second Adam) was blessed in being the firstfruit superior to the first person created by God—the first Adam.

11:21 By faith Jacob, when he was dying, blessed each of the sons of Joseph. This refers to the story in Genesis regarding how Jacob blessed Manasseh and Ephraim, his two sons, by placing his hands on each of their heads, crossing his arms and placing his right arm not on the child to his right—Manasseh, the firstborn—but instead on the head of the child to his left—Ephraim, the younger—while placing his left hand on Manasseh (Gen. 48). Joseph actually was *"displeased"* when he saw this and tried correcting his father, taking *"hold of his father's hand to remove it from Ephraim's head to Manasseh's head,"* telling his father, *"Not so, my father, for this one is the firstborn; put your right hand on his head"* (Gen. 48:17-18). *"But his father refused and said, 'I know, my son, I know. He also shall become a people, and he also shall be great; but truly his younger brother shall be greater than he, and his descendants shall become a multitude of nations'"* (Gen. 48:19). This again was an example of how the second Adam, Christ, who has become *"the firstruits of those who have fallen asleep,"* was superior to the first Adam (compared with Ephraim, the second born, who received greater blessing than the firstborn, Manasseh—see commentary on Heb. 11:20 for more on this).

and worshiped, leaning on the top of his staff. The action of crossing his arms further validated the notion that this event signified the salvation of Christ, through the cross. Here, St. Paul uses a very particular word to describe the blessing Jacob provided for Joseph's two sons: *"worshipped."* It is as if he saying that when Jacob made the sign of the cross with his arms (see Gen. 48:13), he believed and worshipped Christ who would eventually die on the cross. Hence, by faith, Jacob saw the coming of the Messiah and His crucifixion.

11:22 By faith Joseph, when he was dying, made mention of the departure of the children of Israel, and gave instructions concerning his bones. Joseph told them: *"'I am dying; but God will surely visit you, and bring you out of this land to the land of which He swore to Abraham, to Isaac, and to Jacob.' Then Joseph took an oath from the children of Israel, saying, 'God will surely visit you, and you shall carry up my bones from here'"* (Gen. 50:24-25). So, Joseph believed in the promise even without seeing its fulfillment. He instructed them, in confidence regarding this promise, that when they eventually leave Egypt to go to the promised land, they should take his bones with them. Believing in the exodus of Israel symbolized the belief in our deliverance from Satan through Christ.

11:23-29 In this set of verses, St. Paul will elaborate about the faith of Moses, who was and still is a great figure in the eyes of the Jews. Remember that St. Paul is addressing Christians from a Jewish origin. That is why he elaborated on the faith related to Moses, mentioning various points as explained below.

11:23 By faith Moses, when he was born, was hidden three months by his parents, because they saw he was a beautiful child; and they were not afraid of the king's command. Some people will question, where is their faith here? They hid their child, so how does that exemplify faith? The faith was demonstrated in two things. First, when they saw that he was a beautiful child, they saw God's blessing on him, being able to see that this baby would be a deliverer of Israel from the land of Egypt. So, they did not just see *"a beautiful child,"* but also that he was a special child from God. The second manner in which their action demonstrates their faith is that they were not afraid that the child would die, as Pharaoh had commanded, but rather had faith that God would protect their child Moses. St. Paul is telling them then that faith makes us brave and gives us courage. Trusting in God allows us to stand *"before kings and rulers"* for the sake of Christ (Luke 21:12). Faith *"casts out fear"* (1 John 4:18) from our hearts. Fear is a sign of unbelieving.

11:24-25 By faith Moses, when he became of age, refused to be called the son of Pharaoh's daughter, choosing rather to suffer affliction with the people of God than to enjoy the passing pleasures of sin. These two verses have a beautiful message for our youth. Many children come regularly to the church simply because their parents bring them. But when they grow up, they decide not to come to church, and when parents implore that they attend church, their child or children are unwilling. Here, St. Paul is highlighting the positive choices that Moses made when he *"became of age."* He chose not *"to be called the son of Pharaoh's daughter."* He refused the status and prestige that came along with being regarded like a prince of Egypt. Instead, he chose *"to suffer affliction with the people of God."* Sometimes because of peer pressure, we conform to the ways of the world, not wanting to suffer in the same manner of affliction as the people of God, having to refrain from worldly ways as they do. Moreover, Moses chose also not *"to enjoy the passing pleasures of sin."* As a youth, he did not choose to please himself with the passing pleasures of sin. And here I have a question to all our youth: as you are growing up, what choices are you making? Are you making choices like Moses or like the people of the world? Are you going to be identified with the people of God or the people of the world. Moses refused to be identified with the children of the world, choosing instead to be identified among the people of God. Here, St. Paul is saying something very clear: you cannot have a happy medium between God and the world. You cannot keep a middle ground between the two. And to choose one means you reject the other. *"No one can serve two masters; for either he will hate the one and love the other, or else he will be loyal to the one and despise the other"* (Matt. 6:24). You choose either to be among the people of God or the children of the world. Loving the world is enmity with God. Are you willing to risk your life, status, privilege, financial security, material possessions, and pleasure of sin for Christ? Moses was willing to lose all of these things for Christ.

11:26 esteeming the reproach of Christ greater riches than the treasures in Egypt; for he looked to the reward. Here, St. Paul explains why Moses was willing to forego all of the pleasures of a worldly life. St. Paul here alludes to his previous mention (in Heb. 11:6) about how God is *"a rewarder of those who diligently seek Him."* The message here is then, to suffer for Christ and to lose for Christ is better than enjoying and gaining the passing pleasures of this passing world. Where is your focus? Are you focusing on the seen or the unseen? Faith focuses on the unseen. Are you focusing on what is temporal or what is eternal? Moses focused on the eternal reward, not the temporal one.

11:27 By faith he forsook Egypt, not fearing the wrath of the king. Moses actually left Egypt twice. The first time, he left because he *"feared"* the king, having killed an Egyptian (Ex. 2:12-14). But this verse does not refer to this incident. St. Paul is referring to the exodus from Egypt when Moses and Aaron courageously, and not in fear, confronted Pharaoh and asked him to let the Israelites go to worship God in the wilderness.

for he endured as seeing Him who is invisible. Moses trusted in the protection of God. That is why this trust caused him to endure courageously during his confrontations with Pharaoh, as if Moses saw God, the invisible. But that is faith: *"evidence of things not seen"* (Heb. 11:1).

11:28 he who destroyed. This refers to the angel who *"struck all the firstborn in the land of Egypt"* (Ex. 12:29). .

By faith he kept the Passover and the sprinkling of blood, lest he who destroyed the firstborn should touch them. Again here, Moses trusted God, that if he kept the Passover, God would protect the firstborn of the Israelites. He believed that by sprinkling the blood of the Passover lamb, the angel would not kill the firstborn of Jews.

11:29 By faith they passed through the Red Sea as by dry land, whereas the Egyptians, attempting to do so, were drowned. Not only did Moses obey and have faith in God, but also all the Israelites, who were at first reluctant and grumbled against Moses saying, *"have you taken us away to die in the wilderness ... let us alone that we may serve the Egyptians, for it would have been better for us to serve the Egyptians than that we should die in the wilderness"* (Ex. 14:11-12). But after this, they believed God. When the Egyptians, who lacked faith, attempted to enter onto the dry land to pass through the Red Sea, they died. What saved the Israelites and not the Egyptians was their faith. St. Paul is encouraging the Hebrews to risk their lives for Christ as their great prophet Moses did. Obedience is a sign of faith. But when we do not obey, we enter into a vicious cycle that continues to weaken our faith. Disobeying God creates guilt in us; this guilt will cause us to feel reluctant in trusting God because we are unworthy; and then suck lack of trust will lead us to more disobedience. Instead, through faith, we should interrupt this cycle and know that, even if there are moments in life in which we lack faith or are disobedient, if we return to God, He will forgive and protect us.

11:30-38 After speaking about Moses, St. Paul gives other examples of faith. By this point, St. Paul has probably already done enough to make clear the point he was trying to make, that faith gives us courage, endurance, perseverance, and without faith we cannot please God or receive salvation. St. Paul will thus, not dwell in speaking about any one character from the Bible in this next set of verses, but rather briefly mention the manner in which their faith was exhibited.

11:30 By faith the walls of Jericho fell down after they were encircled for seven days. God asked the Israelites to encircle the walls of Jericho, but it was definitely not such encirclement that caused the walls to fall down. You can encircle any city for as many years as you want and its walls will not fall. But they trusted that God, who is faithful, will fulfill His promises. This was then a sign of their faith that was demonstrated through their obedience.

11:31 By faith the harlot Rahab did not perish with those who did not believe, when she had received the spies with peace. St. Paul here is referring to what Rahab said to the two spies: *"I know that the Lord has given you this land"* (Joshua 2:9). She expressed faith in God, and because of this, she believed. The rest of the city, who did not believe, perished.

11:32 **And what more shall I say? For the time would fail me to tell of Gideon and Barak and Samson and Jephthah, also of David and Samuel and the prophets.** St. Paul is saying here, "What more can I tell you? To explain for you the faith demonstrated through Scripture among the heroes of the Old Testament, I would need much more time." He mentions here four judges, one king, and also one prophet (Samuel) who was also considered to be a judge. St. Paul, by simply mentioning the names of these people, is in this way, giving them some "homework" for them to do: that they contemplate on these people's faith.

11:33 **who through faith subdued kingdoms, worked righteousness, obtained promises.** St. Paul begins now to summarize what the heroes of faith (mentioned in the previous verse) did. These first three actions can be applied to all the judges mentioned.

stopped the mouths of lions. This can be applied to Samson (Judg. 14) and David (1 Sam. 17:34-37), who both killed lions, and also to Daniel (Dan. 6).

11:34 **quenched the violence of fire.** This applies to Shadrach, Meshach, and Abed-nego (Dan. 3) who were thrown into the furnace of fire but came out alive.

escaped the edge of the sword, out of weakness were made strong, became valiant in battle, turned to flight the armies of the aliens. All of these descriptions can be applied to the judges and also to David the king and prophet.

11:35 **Women received their dead raised to life again.** Here St. Paul is referring to Elijah (1 Kings 17-18) and Elisha (2 Kings 4), who each raised the dead son of a widow.

Others were tortured, not accepting deliverance, that they might obtain a better resurrection. St. Paul introduces another concept: in the resurrection, there will be different ranks, as one star will differ from other stars in glory (1 Cor. 15:41). So are you looking to just enter into the kingdom of heaven, or a better resurrection? These people had opportunity to be delivered, but they did not accept deliverance, in order to obtain a *"better resurrection"* and more glory. Many of us just follow the minimum requirements to enter into heaven, being content to simply enter. But here, St. Paul says, "No, we should look for not just resurrection, but a better resurrection, to be glorified with Christ." That is why these people did not accept deliverance. Do we have the mentality of following the minimum requirements to enter into heaven, or are we trying to excel there? Here on earth, no one wants the minimum, but everyone usually seeks to be promoted in life. How come when it comes to heaven, people are comfortable to be last. Here, people seek the best in a world that is temporary, but in heaven, they accept the least in a world that is eternal.

11:36 **Still others had trial of mockings and scourgings, yes, and of chains and imprisonment.** The apostles suffered such things.

11:37 **They were stoned.** St. Stephen was stoned to death (Acts 7:59-60).

they were sawn in two. This refers to Isaiah the prophet and his manner of death.

were tempted, were slain with the sword. St. Paul is trying to make clear that faith is no protection against persecution. Some people think that if they believe in God, they should not expect to suffer. On the contrary, when you believe, you will receive strength to endure suffering.

They wandered about in sheepskins and goatskins, being destitute, afflicted, tormented. This is like Elijah (2 Kings 1:8) and St. John the Baptist (Matt. 3:4; Mark 1:6).

11:38 **of whom the world was not worthy.** This is a truly wonderful description. For the heroes of faith, such as those mentioned previously, were considered to be so magnificent in their exhibition of faith that the world is not a good enough place to deserve them living in it. Only heaven truly befits their faithfulness under such horrible persecution and the pressures that they suffered.

They wandered in deserts and mountains, in dens and caves of the earth. One may think of monks today as they read this verse.

11:39 **And all these, having obtained a good testimony through faith, did not receive the promise.** St. Paul again emphasizes that such people as those mentioned previously were able to live a life of trust and confidence in God even without experiencing fulfillment of the promise of God. Note though here that St. Paul speaks of *"the promise"* in the singular sense. That is because while there are many promises made by God, all are fulfilled through Christ. Hence, all the heroes of the Old Testament obtained a good testimony from God that they were righteous because of their faith although they did not experience Christ. He is imploring the Hebrews to then consider how much more they, who are Christians and have received the Holy Spirit, should live lives in a faithful way.

11:40 God having provided something better for us. God provided something better for us Christians when He sent His only begotten Son to the world to save us and give us His eternal inheritance in the kingdom of heaven.

that they should not be made perfect apart from us. This reminds me of what is written in the Book of Revelation (6:10-11), when the souls of those who were killed because of their testimony about God cried out, *"How long, O Lord, holy and true, until You judge and avenge our blood on those who dwell on the earth?"* They were asked to wait *"a little while longer,"* each being given *"a white robe,"* until the death of all the believers *"was completed."* God did not perfect or glorify the Old Testament heroes of faith and sufferers of persecution, giving them the ultimate fulfillment of the promise (which is the inheritance of the kingdom of God), because we are all one body, one Church, and He was waiting for all of us to be glorified together.

Chapter 11 Questions

1. What difference does it make whether or not you believe God will reward "those who diligently seek Him"? (v. 6)

2. What would be the characteristics of a believer who lived his life as a "pilgrim" and "stranger" here on earth?

3. How does faith affect our willingness to suffer?

4. How does faith deal with instant gratification?

12

Chapter Outline

- Imitating the Lord (1-4)
- Discipline (5-11)
- The call to holiness (12-17)
- Pilgrimage of the new covenant (18-24)
- Fifth warning: danger of refusing God (25-29)

Introduction

St. Paul, addressing the Hebrews that were being tempted to return back to Judaism, emphasizes in this chapter the importance of obedience even under such pressure.

12:1 Therefore we also, since we are surrounded by so great a cloud of witnesses ... and let us run with endurance the race that is set before us. St. Paul likens the persecution the Hebrews were facing to return back to Judaism to a race, which they need to run with endurance—that is, by remaining faithful with Christ until the end. What will motivate them and support them in their attempt to accept all such suffering? *"We are surrounded by so great a cloud of witnesses."* He is referring to the heroes of faith he mentioned in the previous chapter, who were able to run the race and remain faithful to God without receiving the fulfillment of the promises, having died beforehand. Now, being surrounded by this cloud of witnesses, knowing that so many people before us were able to run the race and finish it, we are motivated to follow in their footsteps. Moreover, these saints are a support system: for example, I know that St. Mary, St. Mark, St. George are praying for me.

surrounded. This means the saints are not far from us. They can hear us, and therefore, can pray for us..

so great. When we know that the number of the witnesses on our behalf are *"so great,"* we know that there were many people who were heroes of faith and were able to finish the race. As they were able, so too are we motivated and have an assurance in our hope to also be capable of finishing the race.

cloud. He uses this word, signifying the fact that they are now in the Paradise of Joy above us. Also, notice that he used the singular word here for *"cloud,"* implying that we are one Church, and one Body of Christ.

witnesses. They witnessed to the Lord during their lives. Also, they are watching us right now and, knowing our needs and understanding our weaknesses, they continually support us with their prayers. As Christ said, *"'I am the God of Abraham, the God of Isaac, and the God of Jacob'? God is not the God of the dead, but of the living"* (Matt. 22:32). This cloud of witnesses are alive, watching us and praying for us all of the time.

let us lay aside every weight. It is not enough to run our race with simply "a cloud of witnesses." If you run a race, you will be slowed down if you are carrying heavy weights along with you. St. Paul here distinguishes between *"weight"* and *"sin."* Weight does not necessarily refer to something sinful, but can nonetheless be something that hinders us from running the race and following the Lord Christ. An example may be taken from the parable of the sower, when Christ said that a person may be hindered by the *"thorns"* of this world, which are *"the cares of this world and the deceitfulness of riches"* which *"choke the word"* of God, whereby a person *"becomes unfruitful"* (Matt. 13:22). We need to examine ourselves: what things hold us back from running the race?

and the sin which so easily ensnares us. Aside from laying aside every *"weight,"* which can signify things other than sin, in order to run our race, we need to refrain from sin. Maybe in St. Paul's mind he was thinking of apostasy, speaking of *"the sin"* in a singular sense. Or maybe he uses the singular form of this word to indicate that any sin is a sin, so that a person can read this as saying we need to refrain from every sin. Note that St. Paul, over the course of this epistle, describes sin in three ways: (1) it is deceitful (Heb. 3:13; and as it is also mentioned elsewhere in this commentary, including Heb. 3:13), because the power of Satan lies in his ability to deceive, and if he loses his ability to deceive us, he becomes powerless, as it is said in the Divine Liturgy, *"and when we fell by the deception of the Serpent"*; (2) the pleasure of sin will pass away (Heb. 11:25), being temporary and fleeting in the gratification we receive from it; (3) and also, sin was described as being able to easily ensnare us, so that if you are not watchful and remain fixed on the Lord Christ, sin is ready to hold us captive (and if you are trapped by sin, you cannot run your race).

12:2 looking unto Jesus, the author and finisher of our faith ... and has sat down at the right hand of the throne of God. This verse provides us motivation for running the race and remaining Christian in the face of persecution. The Lord Christ is very different than the heroes of faith mentioned in the previous chapter and of whom were spoken as a means of motivation in the previous verses. Not only is Christ a *"hero of faith"* but He is also *"the author finisher of our faith."* The Lord Christ is the one who started our journey to the kingdom of heaven, and he finished the journey (being seated at the right hand of God). He is the only person about whom we can say started and also finished the journey. When we fix our eyes on the Lord Jesus Christ who started and finished the journey of faith, we will be motivated to finish the race ourselves.

who for the joy that was set before Him endured the cross, despising the shame. St. Paul tells us that the Lord Jesus Christ *"endured"* the cross and despised the shame because of *"the joy that was set before Him."* He had joy in fulfilling His mission, saving humanity, crushing Satan, trampling upon death, and saving us from the bondage of sin. Because of the joy in all of these things, He endured the cross and despised the shame. Many times we focus on our cross, which makes us often become weary by its magnitude and weight. If instead we concentrate on the joy in the resurrection that comes after the cross, then we can endure and despise the shame of our cross. (Think of the story when the disciples were afraid of the wind and the sea while they were in the boat, who were afterward amazed at the fact that same wind and sea of which they were afraid obeyed Christ's command—Matt. 8:27; Mark 4:41; Luke 8:25). Fixing our eyes on Christ, *"looking unto Jesus,"* we will be able to endure until the end and finish our race.

12:3-4 **For consider Him who endured such hostility from sinners against Himself, lest you become weary and discouraged in your souls. You have not yet resisted to bloodshed, striving against sin.** When you go through difficult times and suffer for Christ, another manner of motivation is to consider the pains and sufferings Christ went through and the price He had to pay as compared with our pains and the very little price we have to pay in order to endure. All the suffering we endure is not at all comparable to the blood shed on the cross by Christ. He suffered the punishment of a sinner although He is the holy one. Reflecting on the suffering of the Lord makes us understand His love and thus, protects us from any temptation. The cost of our salvation was Christ's blood; but the price of our faithfulness is usually not bloodshed. In spite of this, we still complain of the difficulties and tribulations that befall us as we follow in *"the Way"* (Acts 9:2). God expects us to strive against sin to the point of bloodshed if necessary.

12:5-6 **And you have forgotten the exhortation which speaks to you as to sons.** God exhorts us as children, not as slaves, to endure tribulation. Many people think that the children of God should not suffer. St. Paul reminds us with what was written in Proverbs 3:11-12:

"**My son, do not despise the chastening of the LORD, nor be discouraged when you are rebuked by Him; for whom the LORD loves He chastens, and scourges every son whom He receives.**" St. Paul is telling us here that God, as a true father, because of His love, uses suffering as an opportunity to discipline us. Suffering does not come from God. For example, the persecution being suffered by the Hebrews, pressuring them to return to Judaism, was not from God. Instead, such suffering is an opportunity for discipline. Such discipline is essential in developing our faith and for spiritual maturity. When the Lord disciplines us, we should not be angry, be upset, or complain. Discipline is a sign of love, for it happens to *"whom the Lord loves."*

astray? Your son will be given your due attention because you would not discipline a stranger. Hence, discipline is a sign of our authentic relationship with God, and when we accept such discipline, God will deal with us as children. Not only is discipline a sign of an authentic relationship with God, but it makes us aware that we are like God's children. The prodigal son, when he left his home, was not treated like a son until he returned. In a similar way, we can understand that when we accept God's discipline, we are accepting being God's children and accepting His fatherhood. If you accept discipline, you are a son, but if you do not, you are *"illegitimate."* Knowing that discipline is a sign of God's love and an indication of our relationship with him as children, we should accept his discipline with gratitude.

12:7-8 **If you endure chastening, God deals with you as with sons; for what son is there whom a father does not chasten? But if you are without chastening, of which all have become partakers, then you are illegitimate and not sons.** When an earthly father sees their children going astray, they discipline them. If they did not do so, that means the father does not care about his children. Moreover, think about this: if there are two children, one is your son, the other is a stranger, which one will you discipline if both are going

12:9 **Furthermore, we have had human fathers who corrected us, and we paid them respect. Shall we not much more readily be in subjection to the Father of spirits?** Think about how we treat our own fathers. (St. Paul implies here the notion that our human fathers care for our bodies, while our divine Father cares for our spirits). If we pay respect to our earthly fathers, we should definitely pay respect to our heavenly Father.

and live. We have read previously that discipline is a sign of love, genuine sonship, and if we do not accept such discipline, we are no longer children of God, but rather illegitimate. However, what is the fruit of our discipline? The first fruit is life, for those who accept God's discipline.

12:10 **For they.** That is, our human fathers.

indeed for a few days chastened us as seemed best to them, but He for our profit, that we may be partakers of His holiness. While earthly fathers discipline us for a very short while, God disciplines us for our own profit so that *"we may be partakers of His holiness."* Heeding God's discipline does not only result in eternal life with Him, but it allows us to be holy like God (*"Be holy, for I am holy"*—Lev. 11:45; *"Therefore you shall be perfect, just as your Father in heaven is perfect"*—Matt. 5:48). If you want to be a holy person, you have to accept the discipline of God.

12:11 **Now no chastening seems to be joyful for the present, but painful; nevertheless, afterward it yields the peaceable fruit of righteousness to those who have been trained by it.** St. Paul understands that accepting suffering, which God uses as a means of disciplining us, is *"painful."* But he reminds them not to look at the cross they have to carry, but rather the joy at the outcome (see Heb. 12:2). The time of discipline is definitely not joyful but painful. However, it yields the *"peaceable fruit of righteousness,"* which means we will be righteous people, experiencing peace in its three dimensions (with others, with God, and with ourselves). Such peace achieved through discipline needs training, which is a continuous process of accepting suffering with gratitude.

12:12-17 In this set of verses, St. Paul calls people to live a holy life. He will teach that in order to endure the race and the pain of discipline, and in order to live a life holiness, we need the support of one another. That is why God created us and "made us unto Himself an assembled people" (as we say in the Divine Liturgy): people who are living in fellowship. You cannot be saved by yourself, because you are made as a part of a whole, being part of the whole Body of Christ. Supporting one another is very important to endure as we run the race and try to live a life of holiness.

12:12 **Therefore strengthen the hands which hang down, and the feeble knees.** St. Paul encourages us to strengthen the weak among us. This verse comes from Isaiah 35:3.

12:13 and make straight paths for your feet, so that what is lame may not be dislocated, but rather be healed. It is not enough to just support the weak, to *"strengthen the hands which hang down, and the feeble knees,"* but it is also not appropriate to put an obstacle in the way of a person who is *"lame"* in their relationship with Christ, who has not healed yet. *"Make straight paths"* means, do not be an obstacle or an offense for one another. This verse was taken from Proverbs 4:26.

12:14 Pursue peace. As Christians, we are bearing the *"peaceable fruit of righteousness"* (Heb. 12:11), and therefore, need to *"pursue peace."* The two fruits of discipline are peace with people and also holiness.

with all people. This is in regard to our relationship with people, rather than with God. *"Blessed are the peacemakers, for they shall be called sons of God"* (Matt. 5:9).

and holiness. This is in regard to our relationship with God.

without which no one will see the Lord. *"Blessed are the pure in heart, for they shall see God"* (Matt. 5:8).

12:15-16 looking carefully lest anyone fall short of the grace of God. We have to support one another because if my brother falls from the grace of God, I will be affected too. If you are weak, I will be weak too. If you are strong, I will be strong too. This is because we are both members of the same body—the Body of Christ. Hence, if any member falls short of the grace of God, we will all be affected. St. Paul gives us an example of someone who fell short of the grace of God in the upcoming verses.

lest any root of bitterness springing up cause trouble, and by this many become defiled; lest there be any fornicator or profane person like Esau, who for one morsel of food sold his birthright. Esau married foreign wives (who did not worship the same God as he was taught to worship), which was against God's commandments, and is, therefore, called here a *"fornicator"* for that reason. He was also *"profane"* because he did not take his birthright seriously. We read in the Book of Genesis, when Esau married these foreign wives, it was a source of bitterness to both his father and mother. Not only that, Esau was a source of bitterness to his brother Jacob, who escaped from Esau's presence. That is why St. Paul says that anyone who falls from the grace of God will be a source of *"bitterness"* to the rest of the Body of Christ. If a person in the church starts to defile himself, he will cause bitterness to the rest of the congregants, and this person may defile others in the church, since *"evil company corrupts good habits"* (1 Cor. 15:33).

12:17   For you know that afterward, when he wanted to inherit the blessing, he was rejected, for he found no place for repentance, though he sought it diligently with tears. Falling from the grace of God will affect our eternal life, as was the case with Esau, who was rejected because he was a *"fornicator"* and a *"profane person"* (previous verse). Despite all of this, if he had repented, he would have received a blessing. However, *"he found no place for repentance."* The phrase *"he sought it diligently with tears"* does not mean that Esau repented. Rather, he sought *"the blessing ... with tears,"* without repentance. Thus, this verse can be read to say he was rejected because he did not repent, although he wished he could have received the blessing irrespective of his lack of repentance. What is *"the blessing"* he sought so diligently to the point of shedding tears? It was the hope that the Messiah would come from his offspring. That is why when Isaac blessed Jacob, Esau asked, *"'Have you only one blessing, my father? Bless me—me also, O my father!' And Esau lifted up his voice and wept"* (Gen. 27:38). Someone may say that Jacob took the blessing by deceit. Yes, however, when Esau came to Isaac and he realized his son Jacob deceitfully took Isaac's blessing, he realized that this was meant to be by God, and therefore, affirmed Jacob's blessing. This affirmation means Esau was rejected. Isaac, by the Holy Spirit, knew that it was God's will that Jacob was given the blessing whereby from his offspring will come the Messiah, telling Esau, *"Indeed I have made him your master ... what shall I do now for you, my son?"* (Gen. 27:37). We learn from all of this that if we do not repent, we will likewise not receive God's blessings.

12:18-21   For you have not come to the mountain that may be touched and that burned with fire, and to blackness and darkness and tempest, and the sound of a trumpet and the voice of words, so that those who heard it begged that the word should not be spoken to them anymore. (For they could not endure what was commanded: "And if so much as a beast touches the mountain, it shall be stoned or shot with an arrow." And so terrifying was the sight that Moses said, "I am exceedingly afraid and trembling.") St. Paul already addressed the theological aspect of his argument regarding the excellence of the new covenant over the old in the first 10 chapters of this epistle; now, as he has been giving practical application of the principles he set forth previously, he tells us that the excellence of the new covenant is another reason why we should run the race until the end. The old covenant was established on Mount Sinai where there was terror and fear (Ex. 19:12-13), because at that time we were not reconciled with God, and therefore, we were His enemies; sin was a barrier between God and us. When God appeared on Mount Sinai, they saw it with *"fire"* and *"blackness and darkness and tempest,"* and they could hear the *"sound of a trumpet"* along with *"thunderings, ... lightning flashes ... and the mountain smoking"* (Ex. 20:18). When people saw, they *"trembled and stood afar off"* (Ex. 20:18). It was so terrifying to the point that people told Moses, go and speak with God and then come back and tell us what He wants from us: *"Then they said to Moses, 'You speak with us, and we will hear; but let not God speak with us, lest we die'"* (Ex. 20:19). Their fear came from the visual spectacle before them as well as *"what was commanded,"* which was that no one or any living thing was allowed to touch the mountain. It was so terrifying that even Moses was terrified, as we read in Deuteronomy 9:19. St. Paul is saying that the old covenant was a covenant of terror and fear. He says that they have not come to all of this, but rather to another more excellent covenant, on which he elaborates in the next few verses.

12:22 But you have come to Mount Zion and to the city of the living God, the heavenly Jerusalem. The old covenant was one accompanied with fear and terror, as it was delivered in a frightening manner on Mount Sinai (Heb. 12:18-21). However, St. Paul tells the Hebrews that they, as Christians, are given the excellence of the new covenant by approaching the heavenly Mount Zion (whose earthly counterpart is a symbol and shadow of the heavenly one), which is the true city in heaven. St. Paul wants them to compare the new covenant and its peaceful and blissful promise of heaven with the old covenant which was filled with terror.

to an innumerable company of angels. If the Jews take pride that they received the law *"through angels"* (Heb. 2:2), how much more should they take pride in Christianity where we not only receive words spoken from angels, but are now in the company of angels. That is why we call the church "the house of angels."

12:23-24 to the general assembly. The "general assembly" of the saints: that is the great cloud of witnesses (Heb. 12:1).

and church of the firstborn. Jacob was not the firstborn, but through his faith in God, the firstborn (Esau) was rejected and the second born received the blessing belonging to the firstborn. St. Paul is saying, when we are faithful to Christ, we will receive the blessing of the firstborn. Every believer, when he believes in Christ and remains faithful to Him until the end, he will receive the blessing of the firstborn.

who are registered in heaven, to God the Judge of all, to the spirits of just men made perfect, to Jesus the Mediator of the new covenant. In the Old Testament, people could not approach God. Even when Moses spoke with God, *"his face shone"* so much that afterward, they needed to *"put a veil on his face"* (Ex. 34:29, 33), which represented the barrier between us and God that existed before Christ. They could not look at his face and *"were afraid to come near him"* (Ex. 34:29). However, now in the era of the New Testament, Christ has opened the way into heaven and allowed us to have *"boldness to enter the Holiest by the blood of Jesus"* (Heb. 10:19). Although we know that God is the Judge of all, we are not terrified. Usually, a person accused of a crime is afraid to stand before the judge; but we are not afraid, knowing that the blood of Jesus Christ cleanses us of every stain of sin. Christ opened the way as our Mediator between us and the Father. That is why we are not terrified to stand before God, the just Judge.

and to the blood of sprinkling that speaks better things than that of Abel. St. Paul is comparing the blood of the Lord Jesus Christ with that of Abel. In the previous chapter, St. Paul mentioned Abel as well, saying, *"By faith Abel offered to God a more excellent sacrifice than Cain, through which he obtained witness that he was righteous, God testifying of his gifts; and through it he being dead still speaks"* (Heb. 11:4). Although he died, he *"still speaks"* as God said to Cain in Genesis, that Abel's blood *"cries out to Me from the ground"* (Gen. 4:10). Let us compare the blood of Abel with the blood of Christ. The blood of Abel spoke a word of hatred between brothers and served as a testimony deserving of condemnation from God. The blood of the Lord Jesus Christ, *"sprinkling"* us from every sin, speaks to us a word of forgiveness (*"In Him we have redemption through His blood, the forgiveness of sins, according to the riches of His grace."*—Eph. 1:7), reconciliation (*"For if when we were enemies we were reconciled to God through the death of His Son, much more, having been reconciled, we shall be saved by His life."*—Rom. 5:10; *"Now all things are of God, who has reconciled us to Himself through Jesus Christ, and has given us the ministry of reconciliation."*—2 Cor. 5:18), love (*"And walk in love, as Christ also has loved us and given Himself for us, an offering and a sacrifice to God for a sweet-smelling aroma."*—Eph. 5:2; *"In this is love, not that we loved God, but that He loved us and sent His Son to be the propitiation for our sins."*—1 John 4:10; *"To Him who loved us and washed* *us from our sins in His own blood ... be glory and dominion forever and ever."*—Rev. 1:5-6), re-creation (i.e., *"Therefore, if anyone is in Christ, he is a new creation; old things have passed away; behold, all things have become new."*—2 Cor. 5:17), life (i.e., through His blood, *"we know that we have passed from death to life."*—1 John 3:14), grace (whereby we receive a new inheritance in heaven, *"to the praise of the glory of His grace, by which He made us accepted in the Beloved."*— Eph. 1:7). Hence, we should run the race with confidence and endure to the end because we have come to a better covenant—the covenant of Christ.

12:25-29 Finally, St. Paul adds his last warning against apostasy. This epistle has five, and in this set of verses, he introduces the fifth. The first four involved warning them about the danger of neglect (2:1-4), unbelief (3:7-19), not maturing (5:11-14), and shrinking back (10:26-31). The fifth warning is about the danger of refusing God. After the Hebrews have learned all these things about which he has previously spoken, which choice will they make? Deny Christ and return back to Judaism, or remain faithful to Christ? Are you going to deny Him and return to a life of sin or remain steadfast in following Him?

12:25 See that you do not refuse Him who speaks. Be careful. Do not refuse God. He speaks to you now. Notice that St. Paul uses the present tense here, indicating that God speaks to us every day, such as whenever we read His word in the Bible and every time we come to church.

For if they did not escape who refused Him who spoke on earth. Remember that the children of Israel expressed to Moses, in a sense, a refusal to hear *"Him who spoke on earth"* in that they did not want to listen to God, but preferred to hear it from Moses (Ex. 20:19). They *"did not escape"* the wrath of God because they did not listen to Him. They also *"refused Him"* when they turned to the worship of idols, molding from themselves a golden calf (Ex. 32).

much more shall we not escape if we turn away from Him who speaks from heaven. The old covenant was made *"on earth,"* whereas the second covenant was made in heaven, because now the door and way to heaven is open for us. In the old covenant, God spoke with terror on Mount Sinai, but in the new covenant, God speaks with grace from His heavenly throne. Sometimes people like to compare between God of the Old Testament and the God of the New Testament, claiming that the former was harsh while the latter was kind. That is definitely wrong. God of the Old Testament and of the New Testament are one and the same God.

He *"is the same yesterday, today, and forever"* (Heb. 13:8). St. Paul is saying, *"if they did not escape... we [shall] not escape,"* which means, God of the Old Testament is the same as God of the New Testament. *"Our God is a consuming fire"* still, as St. Paul says at the conclusion of this chapter (v. 29). The same God of fire of the Old Testament is the same God of the New Testament. His fire will purify the faithful but destroy the unfaithful. There is one God of both Testaments and both His love and wrath are consistent throughout both.

12:26 whose voice then shook the earth. We read in Exodus 19:18 that the "whole mountain quaked greatly" when *"the Lord descended"* upon Mount Sinai *"in fire."* St. Paul refers to this here.

but now He has promised, saying, "Yet once more I shake not only the earth, but also heaven." In the new covenant, God does not only shake earth, but also heaven. This means that this present heaven and earth will eventually pass away. As St. John says, he *"saw a new heaven and a new earth, for the first heaven and the first earth had passed away"* (Rev. 21:1). See also Hag. 2:6; Is. 2:19, 21, and 13:13).

12:27 Now this, "Yet once more," indicates the removal of those things that are being shaken, as of things that are made, that the things which cannot be shaken may remain. St. Paul refers to Haggai 2:6 which says *"Once more ... I will shake heaven and earth."* The *"things that are being shaken"* refers to those things that are created, like this present heaven and earth. But the *"things which cannot be shaken"* refers to the eternal kingdom of heaven. Christ will remove *"things that are being shaken"* (i.e., this heaven and earth) while the *"things which cannot be shaken"* (i.e., the heavenly realities—the new heaven and the new earth) will remain.

12:28 Therefore, since we are receiving a kingdom which cannot be shaken. In heaven we receive a true inheritance. Notice that St. Paul says, *"we are receiving a kingdom"* in the present continuous sense. This means that, to some degree, when we were baptized and received chrismation, and when we take communion, we, in some sense, *"are receiving"* the *"kingdom"* now.

let us have grace. This means we should have gratitude and thanksgiving as a response to the kingdom that God has given us.

by which we may serve God acceptably with reverence and godly fear. Since we have received a "kingdom which cannot be shaken" from God, our response should be to give God acceptable worship with reverence and godly fear.

12:29 **For our God is a consuming fire.** See commentary on Heb. 11:25: *"much more shall we not escape if we turn away from Him who speaks from heaven."*

Chapter 12 Questions

1. How should believers run the race? What should be their motives?

2. How do you avoid becoming weary?

3. What are the benefits of discipline to the Christian?

4. What is the importance of fellowship?

5. What is godly fear? How does godly fear fit within 1 John 4:18?

13

Chapter Outline

- Love (1-7)
  - Brotherly love (1)
  - Love of strangers (2-3)
  - Love in marriage (4-6)
  - Love of pastors and shepherds (7)

- Warning against heretics (8-9)
- Christian sacrifices (10-16)
- Exhortations and benediction (17-21)
- Final notes and remarks (22-25)

Introduction

In Chapter 12, St. Paul explained to the Hebrews the importance of remaining faithful to Christ. The fact that the Hebrews were facing persecution and different sorts of trials moved St. Paul to offer them pastoral advice in this chapter about how to stay united and pull together in the face of their difficulty. True fellowship is an essential element in facing hardships. People need visible support (our fellow Christians) and invisible support (the Holy Spirit, the angels, and the cloud of witnesses surrounding us). Note also that the closing section of this letter—this chapter—is very similar to the final chapters in the letters of St. Paul, which helps support the notion of St. Paul's authorship of this letter.

13:1-7 St. Paul implores the Hebrews to have true fellowship with each other. There is no true fellowship without love, and so he speaks about different aspects of love: brotherly love, love of strangers, love in marriage, and love of our pastors and shepherds.

13:1 Let brotherly love continue. Before the ascension of the Lord Jesus Christ to heaven, He said to His disciples, *"By this all will know that you are My disciples, if you have love for one another"* (John 13:35). In order to bear witness for Christ and prove to the world that we are Christ's children, we have to exhibit brotherly love. *"God is love, and he who abides in love abides in God, and God in him"* (1 John 4:16). If we do not have love among us in the church, then God does not exist among us, for *"he who does not love does not know God, for God is love"* (1 John 4:8). Brotherly love is what is needed to endure hardships.

13:1 Do not forget to entertain strangers, for by so doing some have unwittingly entertained angels. St. Paul here is referring to a story in the Book of Genesis when Abraham was sitting at the door of his tent (Gen. 18). Three men passed by him and he set out food for them. It turned out that these three men were actually God and two angels. Abraham did not know that he was *"unwittingly"* entertaining angels. Here, St. Paul is encouraging people to be hospitable, to entertain strangers. This was especially important during the early church because many people were being persecuted or were thrown out of their houses or homelands and needed shelter and support. Entertaining strangers is also an opportunity to evangelize. Recall the story of St. Pakhom who was not Christian but, because he was received with hospitality by Christians in upper Egypt during his time in the army, he converted to Christianity (for more on this saint, see "The Story of Christianity in Egypt, Book I, by Iris Habib el Masri, p. 212). During the early years of Christianity, entertaining strangers also provided the opportunity to spread the news of other churches and Christians all over the world. Moreover, by entertaining strangers, they may even get the opportunity to host an apostle who had seen the Lord Christ personally. This letter was written in the first century, and so therefore, maybe someone they would have hosted had seen Christ and could tell about it.

13:3 Remember the prisoners as if chained with them. The Hebrews were facing persecution. Some of them were in prison. St. Paul encouraged their fellow Hebrews to show love to those who are in prison or are being tortured because they have to remember that they could have been in their situation easily, since so many people were suffering such persecution. St. Paul is also reminding them of Christ's commandment, when He said, *"I was a stranger and you did not take Me in, naked and you did not clothe Me, sick and in prison and you did not visit Me"* (Matt. 24:42).

those who are mistreated—since you yourselves are in the body also. Many people were being persecuted at that time. St. Paul says to them that they, being *"in the body,"* can still face the same persecution as their brethren too. So, St. Paul wants the Hebrews to take advantage of their time and opportunity to attend to those who are being mistreated while they have the chance, as they themselves may face the same fate soon. They should, therefore, do unto others as they would like to have done unto them.

13:4 Marriage is honorable among all, and the bed undefiled; but fornicators and adulterers God will judge. During the time of the writing of this epistle, there were many who were claiming that marriage, as well as eating meat, is a sin. St. Paul was supporting Christians against this heresy, indicating that marriage is honorable as a Mystery established by God when He created Eve for Adam, and was also blessed when Christ attended and blessed the wedding of Cana of Galilee (John 2). The relationship between husband and wife is undefiled, because God Himself—the Holy Spirit—causes this union; it is not a union effectuated simply by a judge who agrees to acknowledge the joining of two people in marriage. St. Paul wants to remind the Hebrews to keep God in their midst, especially during the time of persecution. If people began to abrogate from the sanctity of marriage, God would remove His blessings and presence from them.

13:5-6 Let your conduct be without covetousness; be content with such things as you have. For He Himself has said, "I will never leave you nor forsake you." So we may boldly say: "The LORD is my helper; I will not fear. What can man do to me?" As explained in Chapter 11 previously, some Christians were facing the loss of possessions and money. St. Paul is comforting them here by telling them not to be covetous of the unbelievers (because they did not lose their money), but rather to be content with the little money that they have. Do not grieve the loss of your money for the sake of Christ. God promised us that He will never leave us or forsake us. That is why we, the believers, who are exceedingly confident in God, can say boldly, *"The Lord is my helper, I will not fear. What can man do to me?"* As long as we are under the hand of God and His protection, we have nothing to fear. St. Paul is telling them that, therefore, love and utter dependence on money (rather than God) is evil, so they should not worry if they lose their possessions for Christ's sake because God will take care of them.

13:7 Remember those who rule over you. *"Those who rule over you"* refers to the pastors and shepherds of the church. If you read the history of the church, usually the first people who would be killed as a result of persecution in a particular location would be the clergy. They thought that if they attacked the head of the churches, such as the bishop or the priest, they would be able to weaken the flock because they have killed its main line of support. That is why St. Paul is asking them to show love towards their clergy—their pastors—both those who have departed and also those who are still alive. In the Divine Liturgy, we pray the commemoration of the saints and say, *"As this, O Lord, is the command of Your only-begotten Son, that we share in the commemoration of Your saints."* Many people ask, when did the Lord command us to remember the saints? We know that every word is written by the inspiration of the Holy Spirit, and so the commandments of the apostles are the commandments of God Himself. So, when St. Paul says to *"remember those who rule over you,"* we read this as if God is saying it. So, the answer to the question about where in the Bible it is commanded that we share in the commemoration of the saints, it is this verse.

who have spoken the word of God to you. We should remember, honor, and revere those who have taught us about God, preached to us in His name, and evangelized for His glory.

whose faith follow, considering the outcome of their conduct. St. Paul is here giving us a very important lesson: not only to listen to the teachings of pastors and shepherds, but also to learn from their example. We should consider the end result of their actions and how their faithfulness brought many fruits to the Church of God and to Christ. For the departed, we should reflect on the outcome of their manner of life. This verse also attests to the notion of honoring and venerating saints. This is a commandment in the Bible.

13:8 Jesus Christ is the same yesterday, today, and forever. What does St. Paul mean by this? This is a very important verse and a very needed word of support. The Lord Christ is our protection against persecution and heretical teachings infringing on our faith. Reflecting on this epistle and St. Paul's emphasis on Christ as our High Priest, He performed His duties *"yesterday"* in the sense that He offered up His body as a sacrifice and offered supplications on our behalf— Heb. 5:7), He continues until *"today"* as High Priest by standing at the right Hand of God with His blood in the Holy of the Holies, representing us in front of the Father (Heb. 7:25), and Christ is also a High Priest *"forever"* in that He will never abandon His role as High Priest, as *"He always lives to make intercession for"* us (Heb. 7:25). When we understand that the Lord Jesus Christ who shed His blood for us yesterday, and who is standing by His blood in the Holy of the Holies before the Father interceding for us, and who will never abandon His role as High Priest, we know that we have a continual source of support in Him so that truly we can say, *"The LORD is my helper; I will not fear. What can man do to me?"* (Heb. 13:6).

13:9 Do not be carried about with various and strange doctrines. For it is good that the heart be established by grace, not with foods which have not profited those who have been occupied with them. There were two doctrines in particular that were heretical yet prevalent at the time this epistle was being written. In verse 4, St. Paul responded to the heresy that marriage is abominable. In this verse, St. Paul addresses the improper doctrine that taught people to refrain from eating certain foods, such as meat. St. Paul teaches them, however, that the Hebrews should *"not be carried about* *with various and strange doctrines."* The wrong doctrines about food is different than the teachings about fasting. When we fast, we abstain from eating meat and eat just vegetables, but this is not done because eating meat defiles the body; rather, we refrain from eating meat to discipline the body, as St. Paul says, *"I discipline my body and bring it into subjection, lest, when I have preached to others, I myself should become disqualified"* (1 Cor. 9:27). Meat is not evil or wrong to eat, as during the feasts of the Church we celebrate by eating it. The teachings related to fasting are, thus, completely different than the wrong doctrines promulgated at that time against eating meat, which taught that meat was a source of defilement to one's body. St. Paul tried explaining to them how such a belief does not bring anyone any advantage, but rather, it is the grace of God that strengthens the heart. As he instructed to accept marriage as being honorable, he also instructs them here to accept food as a gift of God.

13:10 **We have an altar from which those who serve the tabernacle have no right to eat.** As you know, the priests in the Old Testament were required to eat from the meat of certain sacrifices offered. However, St. Paul is talking here about the Christian altar, on which is the sacrifice of Christ (His body and blood). Jews *"who serve the tabernacle,"* and all non-Christians who have not yet been baptized, *"have no right to eat"* of the Eucharist from the altar of the New Testament.

13:11-12 **For the bodies of those animals, whose blood is brought into the sanctuary by the high priest for sin, are burned outside the camp. Therefore Jesus also, that He might sanctify the people with His own blood, suffered outside the gate.** St. Paul links the rites of the Day of Atonement with the sacrifice of Christ. As we read in Leviticus 16, after the high priest offers the sacrifice on the Day of Atonement and then takes that blood to sprinkle it inside the Holy of the Holies, he then takes the undesirable parts of the sacrifice and brings them outside the camp to burn them. St. Paul is saying that our Lord Jesus Christ was the sacrifice and the High Priest as well. As the High Priest, He entered by His own blood into the Holy of the Holies, which is the heaven of heavens. And as the high priest took the undesirable parts of the body outside of the camp, so too, Christ suffered outside Jerusalem as a sign of reproach, being treated as undesirable. That is why during the Holy Pascha Week we do not pray in the first part of the church but rather pray in the second chorus of the church, as if we are going outside the camp with Christ to share in bearing His reproach. The rites of the Day of Atonement were meant to sanctify the people, and He performed this same rite in a more excellent way to sanctify all of us.

13:13-14 Therefore let us go forth to Him, outside the camp, bearing His reproach. For here we have no continuing city, but we seek the one to come. The Jews threatened that, unless you deny Christ, you will be expelled from the Synagogue. Those who were removed from the Synagogue were aggrieved by this. St. Paul tells such people not to suffer grief, but instead, to willingly *"go forth to Him, outside the camp, bearing His reproach."* If we suffer with Him, we will be glorified with Him as well (Rom. 8:17), and thus, such reproach is actually an honor. St. Paul reminds the Hebrews that when they are cast out of the Synagogue, they are being cast out from a temporary and transitory place—earthly Jerusalem; however, by being removed from there, they must remember that they are members of a heavenly city—heavenly Jerusalem—which is an everlasting city.

13:15 Therefore by Him let us continually offer the sacrifice of praise to God, that is, the fruit of our lips, giving thanks to His name. Acknowledging that we have the honor to be members of the heavenly Jerusalem and not an earthly Jerusalem (which people today still fight over) moves us to offer a *"sacrifice of praise to God."* In the Divine Liturgy, when we chant the hymn, *"Through the intercessions of the Theotokos, Saint Mary, O Lord, grant us the forgiveness of our sins"* we conclude it with the phrase, *"A mercy of peace, a sacrifice of praise."* When we stand before the altar of Christ and the Eucharist and see the sacrifice of His body and blood which opened up for us the way to the heavenly Jerusalem, we offer Him a sacrifice of praise. The term "Eucharist" actually means thanksgiving. We should continually be grateful to God by the fruit of our lips (i.e., with a *"sacrifice of praise"*). The Church Fathers teach that the greatest type of prayer is to praise God. There are many types of prayer (see 1 Tim. 2:1), such as supplications, intercession, etc. Praise, however, is regarded as the most esteemed manner of prayer. This sacrifice of praise is essential in any Divine Liturgy. Before Vespers (the evening offering of incense), we have the Vesper Praises. After Vespers we have the Midnight Praises. Before Matins (the morning offering of incense), we have the Morning Praises. Hence, praise is an essential form of prayer.

13:16 But do not forget to do good and to share, for with such sacrifices God is well pleased. It is not enough to praise God, but thanksgiving must also be translated into deeds of kindness and sharing. St. Paul considered doing good and sharing as a sacrifice. At this point, I want to draw your attention to something very important. Offerings (i.e., contributions to the church) is an essential element of worship. That is why St. Paul taught in 1 Corinthians 16:2, *"On the first day of the week [which is Sunday] let each one of you lay something aside, storing up as he may prosper, that there be no collections when I come."* (Recall that the clergy ask God, during the prayers of the Divine Liturgy, to *"remember ... the sacrifices, the offerings, and the thanksgivings of those who have offered to the honor and glory"* of God. The deacon sings a beautiful special hymn following that prayer, asking the people to pray for such offerings. I am mentioning this because many people make their donations once a year. However, when we understand that offerings are an essential element of worship, then we will think about offering something to God every time we come together for worship. This is biblical. Sometimes only the husband offers on behalf of the family, but St. Paul teaches us (in 1 Cor. 16:2) that *"each one"* should offer.

13:17 Obey those who rule over you, and be submissive, for they watch out for your souls, as those who must give account. St. Paul returns to the notion of honoring and obeying the clergy. The obedience and submission here occurs out of love, not out of fear as with slaves. There are a few reasons given for this: (1) *"for they watch out for your souls,"* which actually describes the function of the bishop, which is a word (episcopos) that literally mans overseer; (2) bishops and priests take their calling very seriously because they must *"give account"* to Christ.

Let them do so with joy and not with grief, for that would be unprofitable for you. By loving and obeying our pastors and shepherds, we allow them to serve us with joy. And when they serve us in this way, it is for our benefit, as we will gain much profit from such service. But if we make them serve us with grief and groaning, that would be *"unprofitable"* for us. If we continuously give our priests and bishops a hard time, they will suffer, and such suffering will reflect on the profitableness of their service to us.

13:18 Pray for us; for we are confident that we have a good conscience, in all things desiring to live honorably. St. Paul wanted to make sure that it is understood that asking the Hebrews to obey and be submissive to the clergy, he is not saying they are superior to them, not needing their support. The clergy need the prayers of the people in order to perform their ministry according to God's plan. That is why in every Divine Liturgy, we pray for the patriarch, the bishops, the priests, the deacons, and the servants. The prayers of the congregation will support the good conscience of the clergy so that they will live honorably. (Notice that St. Paul includes himself in this statement, validating the fact that St. Paul was a bishop.)

13:19 But I especially urge you to do this, that I may be restored to you the sooner. St. Paul now asks for a special prayer for himself. The verb *"restored"* here can refer to healing from an illness, release from prison, or simply refer to ending his absence from them.

13:20 Now may the God of peace who brought up our Lord Jesus from the dead, that great Shepherd of the sheep, through the blood of the everlasting covenant, make you complete in every good work to do His will, working in you what is well pleasing in His sight, through Jesus Christ, to whom be glory forever and ever. Amen. This is what you call the benediction—or the concluding blessing that is being bestowed, such as at the end of the Divine Liturgy.

may the God of peace. St. Paul wants to alert them to the need for peace during times of persecution, and the peace they should seek is that which comes from God, whose peace *"surpasses all understanding"* (Phil. 4:7).

who brought up our Lord Jesus from the dead. God who conquered death and raised the Lord Christ from the dead will also help them conquer the persecution they were facing.

that great Shepherd of the sheep. He reminds them that they are not without protection but under the guidance of the *"good shepherd"* who says that He *"gives His life for the sheep"* (John 10:11).

through the blood of the everlasting covenant. Our great Shepherd Jesus Christ made with us a covenant with His everlasting blood (which St. Paul spoke at length about in Heb. 10).

to whom be glory forever and ever. Amen. When you do the will of God and what is pleasing to Him, there will be glory for Christ forever.

13:22 And I appeal to you, brethren, bear with the word of exhortation, for I have written to you in few words. He humbly urges them to bear with his word and accept his teachings because he cares for them. He is appealing to them to be faithful to Christ and not return back to Judaism. He wants them to accept what he says because he teaches them out of love. The few things that they are reading in St. Paul's letter are nothing in comparison to the glory they will receive if they obey it.

13:23 Know that our brother Timothy has been set free, with whom I shall see you if he comes shortly. Most probably they are telling them that St. Timothy was released from prison. He is sharing with them this good news and his intent to visit them accompanied by St. Timothy.

13:24 Greet all those who rule over you, and all the saints. St. Paul is here sending greetings to the clergy and all the Christians (*"all the saints"*—being sanctified by Christ).

Those from Italy greet you. This can be understood in two ways. If this letter was written while St. Paul was outside of Italy, then he is writing to the Hebrews living in Italy and sending greetings along with Italians that were with him outside of Italy. Otherwise, this verse may imply that St. Paul was in Italy at the time of the writing of his epistle, and therefore, included this greeting from Italians living there to the Hebrews living elsewhere.

13:25 Grace be with you all. Amen. The Hebrews need the grace of God to support them in the persecutions that they were facing.

Chapter 13 Questions

1. How does hospitality to strangers and visiting prisoners related to brotherly love?

2. How can we recognize greed in ourselves? What will the signs indicating this be?

3. What is the antidote for greed in our lives?

4. What kinds of sacrifices or offerings are Christians called upon to make?

Comparison Chart: Atonement / Christ's Sacrifice

Comparison between the Day of Atonement, where a sacrifice would be made for the people, and Christ's sacrifice for all mankind.

Old Testament *Atonement, as described in Lev.16*	New Testament *Correlation to Christ's sacrifice*	Reference(s) *for the NT correlation*
Atonement *Type—symbol, pattern*	Crucifixion *Antitype—fulfillment*	Matt. 27; Mark 15; Luke 23; John 19
"Shadow of..."	...good things to come"	Heb. 10:1
"Copy and shadow of..."	...the heavenly things"	Heb. 8:5
Insufficient	Perfect	Heb. 10:11-12
"Once a year" [repeated yearly] (v.34)	"one sacrifice for sins forever"	Heb 10:12
Atonement for the sins of a single year (v.34)	For all sins at all times for all people "For by one offering He has perfected forever those who are being sanctified."	Heb. 10:14
	"...this He did once for all when He offered up Himself."	Heb. 7:27
Priests: • Many, mortal • Order of Aaron • Atonement for himself (vv.6, 11, 17) • Did not take an oath • Sinful and Weak	• One, continuing forever • Order of Melchizedek • Atone for His people forever • With an oath • "holy, harmless, undefiled, separate from sinners ... higher than the heavens."	Heb. 7:23-24 Heb. 5:5-6 Heb. 4:15; 7:27 Heb. 7:20-21 Heb. 7:26-27
In the Tabernacle (vv.6, 16, 17, 33)	"Greater and more perfect tabernacle, not made with hands."	Heb. 9:11
old covenant, of Moses (v.1)	Better Covenant	Heb. 8:8-13; Jer. 31:31
Preparation required afflicting the soul: humility, fasting, and not working	"My soul is exceedingly sorrowful, even to death." Did not eat for days	Matt. 26:38
Priests take off the elaborate priestly clothes, and put on plain linen clothes (vv.29-31)	"They stripped him" "Humbled Himself and became obedient to the point of death, even the death of the cross."	Matt. 27:28 Phil. 2:8
Most important duty of the high priest	"Now My soul is troubled, and what shall I say? 'Father, save Me from this hour'? But for this purpose I came to this hour."	John 12:27

Orthodox Christian Bible Commentary HEBREWS

CHART (cont'd): *Comparison between the Day of Atonement, where a sacrifice would be made for the people, and Christ's sacrifice for all mankind.*

Old Testament Atonement, as described in Lev.16	New Testament Correlation to Christ's sacrifice	Reference(s) for the NT correlation
Sacrifices: • Many • Blood of goats and calves	• One perfect sacrifice • "Not with the blood of goats and calves, but with His own blood He entered the Most Holy Place once for all, having obtained eternal redemption."	Heb. 10:14 Heb. 9:12 *also see:* 1 Pet. 1:19-20
• Purity (vv.21-22)	• "How much more shall the blood of Christ … cleanse your conscience from dead works."	Heb. 9:14
• Substitutional: innocent animal on behalf of guilty person (vv.21-22)	• "He made Him who knew no sin to be sin for us, that we might become the righteousness of God in Him."	2 Cor. 5:21 *also see:* John 1:29
Shedding of blood needed	"Without shedding of blood there is no remission."	Heb. 9:22
High priest separated in private room in the Tabernacle (vv.14-16, 18, 19)	Holy Passion Week "Indeed the hour is coming .. that you will be scattered, each to his own, and will leave Me alone."	John 16:32
High priest would be up all night	Trial and suffering of the Lord	Matt. 26-27
Presenting the offerings before God at the door of the Tabernacle (v.7)	"Father, 'into Your hands I commit My spirit.'"	Luke 23:46
"Tell Aaron your brother not to come at just any time into the Holy Place inside the veil, before the mercy seat which is on the ark, lest he die; for I will appear in the cloud above the mercy seat" (v.2).	"Then, behold, the veil of the temple was torn in two from top to bottom; and the earth quaked, and the rocks were split, and the graves were opened."	Matt. 27:51-52
Two goats: One killed and one (the scapegoat) let go to a deserted and uninhabited place (vv.8-10, 26)	Death and resurrection God cast away our sins "As far as the east is from the west, so far has He removed our transgressions from us."	1 Pet. 2:24; Heb. 9:28; John 1:29; Is. 53:11 Ps. 103:12
Skin, flesh, and offal burned outside the camp (v.27)	"Jesus also … suffered outside the gate."	Heb. 13:11-14
OUTCOME OF CHRIST'S ATONEMENT "Therefore, brethren, having boldness to enter the Holiest by the blood of Jesus, by a new and living way which He consecrated for us, through the veil, that is, His flesh, and having a High Priest over the house of God, let us draw near with a true heart in full assurance of faith, having our hearts sprinkled from an evil conscience and our bodies washed with pure water. Let us hold fast the confession of our hope without wavering, for He who promised is faithful" (Heb. 10:19-23).		

Chart adapted from one originally created by Father Luke Wassif, hegumen in the Coptic Orthodox Diocese of the Southern United States

www.ingramcontent.com/pod-product-compliance
Lightning Source LLC
Chambersburg PA
CBHW081506040426
42446CB00017B/3415